EXPLO

CHICAGO
BLUES

D1277822

EXPLORING

CHICAGO
BLUES

INSIDE THE SCENE, PAST AND PRESENT

ROSALIND CUMMINGS-YEATES | FOREWORD BY BILLY BRANCH

Charleston London

THE
History
PRESS

Published by The History Press
Charleston, SC 29403
www.historypress.net

Copyright © 2014 by Rosalind Cummings-Yeates
All rights reserved

First published 2014

Manufactured in the United States

ISBN 978.1.62619.322.2

Library of Congress CIP data applied for.

For Alex and all the ancestors who went before

I/am
Just telling
A little/bout what
I/feel
When/you tell
What/you feel and
Tell/it like
You/mean it.
You/singing
Blues.

—*"One Narrator," Sterling D. Plumpp*

Contents

Foreword

On August 20, 1969, the greatest blues festival in history took place. Produced by the legendary Willie Dixon and Murphy Dunne, the son of one of Mayor Richard J. Daley's top political allies, the "Bringing the Blues Back Home" festival boasted an incredible lineup of assorted legendary luminaries, a production that remains unequalled to this day. The promotional poster listed a virtual who's who of Chicago blues talent. According to Jeff Johnson's *Chicago Sun Times* article on June 6, 2004, the featured artists included: Luther Allison, Fred Below, J.T. Brown, Bobby Davis (father of recently slain guitarist Eric Davis), Jimmy Dawkins, Bo Diddley, Sleepy John Estes, Betty Everett, Buddy Guy, John Lee Hooker, Lightnin' Hopkins, Big Walter Horton, Homesick James, Sam Lay, Lafayette Leake, Johnny Littlejohn, Robert Lockwood Jr., Big Mac, Little Milton, Little Brother Montgomery, Otis Spann, Hound Dog Taylor, Koko Taylor, Sonny Thompson, Big Mama Thornton, Muddy Waters, Junior Wells, Howlin' Wolf, Johnny Young and Mighty Joe Young. According to Murphy Dunne, Wolf didn't perform because he was feuding with Muddy at the time and refused to appear on the same bill. Dunne also doesn't recall John Lee Hooker showing up.

It was a day that forged my destiny; it was the first time I'd ever heard the blues. If you can remember the feeling you experienced as a child on the morning of your favorite Christmas, you will know how I felt that day. I was completely blown away. And it still seems incredible to me that, seven years after witnessing the quintessential blues festival produced by Willie Dixon, I became a touring member of Willie Dixon's Chicago Blues All-Stars.

It wasn't long after that I found myself immersed in the depth of the Chicago blues scene, frequenting practically every blues club I could find. At that time, the majority of the clubs were on Chicago's black South Side and West Side neighborhoods—mostly black musicians playing to mostly black audiences—but the blues was also creeping into the whiter North Side and downtown areas, where you find the majority of the clubs today. On any given night, you might catch Junior Wells, Buddy Guy, Lonnie Brooks, Magic Slim, Eddie C. Campbell, Buddy Scott and the Rib Tips, Jimmy Dawkins, J.B. Hutto, James Cotton, Big Walter Horton, Carey Bell, Little Mack Simmons, Son Seals, Johnny Littlejohn, Louis Myers and The Aces, Buster Benton and Foree Superstar. There was the ubiquitous Lefty Dizz, the wild guitar wizard, who often went out of his way to welcome us young cats into the fold. And that was just scratching the surface. The lesser-known but no less talented musicians were also making great music: John Wrencher, Good Rockin' Charles, Necktie Nate, Big Leon Brooks, Arlene Brown, Willie Kent, Bonnie Lee, Johnny Twist, Hip Linkchain and dozens, maybe hundreds, more. And of course, there were the "older cats," established legends such as Homesick James, Kansas City Red, Floyd Jones, Eddie Taylor, Sunnyland Slim, Honey Boy Edwards, Big Red and the venerable boogie-woogie pianist Jimmy Walker, whom I will always fondly remember for giving me my first regular gig in a band. I played with and was welcomed by them all.

I witnessed and participated in a bygone era, a time when each musician and singer was unique in his or her own right. Lefty Dizz was almost as famous for his flamboyant guitar antics as he was for his "Dizzisms." "It's gonna be a mess, I tell ya"; "I'm the Black Tornado"; and "Don't look for me cuz I just might show up!" were just a few of his many trademark utterances. Junior Wells, always dressed to the nines, had his own comical way of delivering a song, sung in a perfect voice—always entertaining, always classically Junior. Big Voice Odom sang with a deepness that took you to church. Hound Dog Taylor defied logic by getting such an incredible tone out of his "made in Japan" guitar, the one with the multicolored plastic buttons. I was always amazed to watch his feet tap simultaneously to the beat of his playing but in opposite directions.

Buddy Guy, Lonnie Brooks, Eddie Shaw, Billy Boy Arnold, Jimmy Johnson, Eddie C. Campbell, Sam Lay and Otis Rush are among the last survivors of their generation in Chicago. I reflect with bitter sweetness on the great times spent in Theresa's, the Checkerboard, Pepper's, Florence's, Artis' and the Queen Bee Lounge—those wonderfully entertaining souls, those cats whose stories would make me laugh till I cried, the guys with whom I would share a half pint, the guys with whom I had the honor of sharing the stage are all but gone.

When I first entered the blues realm, there were relatively few African American musicians of my generation playing the blues in Chicago; most of the young cats by then were white. In retrospect, our appearance at the now historic "New Generation of Chicago Blues" tour, which showcased fifteen of us at the Berlin Jazz Festival in 1977, seems to highlight that fact. Assembled by Jim and Amy O'Neal (founders of *Living Blues* magazine) and accompanied by Willie Dixon, who assumed the role of emcee and patriarch, we were the answer to the question: "Are there any young black musicians playing the blues?" We were enthusiastically received. It is noteworthy to mention that this was the first performance of my band, the Sons of Blues, whose members at that time, except for me, were all sons of important bluesmen.

Although the blues landscape is markedly different today, it is important to acknowledge the participation of the non–African American artists who continue to have a profound impact on the genre. In contrast to the low presence of young black musicians, there was an abundance of young whites who shared a similar passion with me. They were just as apt to be on the bandstand playing as they were in the audience. Make no mistake about it: there *were* great young black players on the scene then, a handful of whom remain active today. Lurrie Bell, Zora Young, Big Time Sarah, Melvin Taylor, Killer Ray Allison, Harmonica Hinds, Johnny B. Moore and Vernon Harrington are still thrilling audiences in Chicago. But the white cats were having a big impact. Harmonica players Paul Butterfield, Charlie Musselwhite and Corky Siegel of the Siegel Schwall Band were already hugely popular by the time I came along. More than a decade later, Stevie Ray Vaughn emerged as the "new Jimi Hendrix" and ushered in a whole new generation of blues fans, many of them white.

I credit Willie Dixon for instilling in me the deep appreciation and love for this significant and neglected African American art form. During my six-year tenure as a member of his band, I learned the importance of the blues as a cultural legacy. This was essential to my role as educator in the Blues in Schools program, which I have taught from 1978 to this day, both domestically and internationally. I incorporate Willie's definition of the blues as "The Facts of Life" in the daily slogan my students recite in every class session and performance. Willie Dixon played an immense part in the blues becoming one of the fundamental catalysts of the British Rock Invasion. It was from Willie that I learned that the blues is the root and all of the rest of America's music is the fruit.

The blues today is a study in contradictions and paradoxes. Although the blues is African American folk music, the majority of the musicians playing it and the majority of the audiences are now white. In my travels around the globe, I encounter skilled musicians and singers from Africa, Europe, Australia, South America and Asia. I have met blues enthusiasts from every corner of the world. Droves of international fans make yearly pilgrimages to festivals, grave sites, birthplaces and blues clubs to pay homage. The majority of these dedicated fans are not wealthy but have been inspired by what I consider the most powerful music on the planet to sacrifice and save their money for the sole purpose of hearing their favorite musicians play live. A multitude of dedicated international musicians also pilgrimage to the blues mecca of Chicago in the hopes that they will have a chance to play with their heroes. An elite few of them, like my pianist Sumito Ariyoshi and Rosa's Lounge owner Tony Mangiullo, have remained here as active musicians. They are just a few examples of the international brotherhood that has been spawned by the blues.

Forty-five years after Willie Dixon's phenomenal blues festival, African American blues fans are now by far the minority of today's audiences. Often, black fans ask where I am playing. When I tell them the club is on the North Side, they respond that the twenty-five-minute drive is too far. I have fans, however, who drove twenty-four hours nonstop from Santiago, Chile, to Buenos Aires, Argentina, to see me perform, sleeping in their car because they didn't have money for a hotel. What an irony: the people whose ancestors created this vibrant art form are the very ones who now rarely hear it, thus finding themselves in the precarious position of denying their own heritage and cultural legacy. Some of us who continue to play the blues for a living are striving to change this cultural disconnect and bring the blues back home.

BILLY BRANCH
January 12, 2014

Acknowledgements

I'd like to thank all of the generous people who helped me with this book, providing information, motivation, support and inspiration. Special thanks to all the people in the blues community who supplied memories, documents and feedback: Sterling Plumpp, Marie Dixon, Billy Branch, Rosa Enrico, Deitra Farr, Eddie Shaw, Erwin Helfer and Tony Manguillo. Thanks to the Columbia College Black Music Research Center for all its expertise and research assistance. Thanks to Floyd Webb, Jacqueline Orange and Greg Parker for their assistance and encouragement. I'd like to thank my parents, Janice and Harry Cummings, for their encouragement and my husband, Andre Reese, and children, Jessamyn and Nathan, for their motivation. And to all the blues musicians, past and present, who sang, played and passed on this vital culture, thank you. Your contributions are appreciated, and your efforts are remembered.

Introduction

I can't remember the first time I heard the blues. As an avid music fan from an early age, I paid attention to all the music swirling around me, from commercial jingles to radio hits and my grandmother's records. But I remember vividly the first time I recognized blues in popular music. I was watching Elvis perform "Hound Dog," and I recognized echoes of the blues in the lyrics, the delivery and the rhythm. Except this music Elvis was singing wasn't exactly what I recalled blues sounding like. I had a murky memory of that same song being belted out by a woman, and it was heavy-hitting and pumped with emotion. It was the blues. But it wasn't until many years later that I would learn blues history and how blues musicians like Big Mama Thornton, who popularized "Hound Dog," would be shoved into the shadows in favor of performers who sang the new, polished form of the genre, called rock 'n' roll. It's significant that this is my first blues memory because I would eventually spend a portion of my journalist career writing about these overlooked artists and championing this music called the blues.

Growing up in Chicago helped me develop an organic appreciation for the blues. Besides the blues history steeped in the very sidewalks of the city, blues floats around everywhere in Chicago. You hear it in restaurants and department stores, on street corners and even at the airports. I always felt proud that the blues was part of my heritage, and I listened closely whenever I heard blues songs on the radio or on TV. When I was old enough, I started hanging out in the city's blues clubs, meeting the musicians, promoters and club owners who drive the Chicago blues scene. This was the '90s, and another blues renaissance was driving national attention to the blues with young artists like Robert Cray and Stevie Ray Vaughn. The Chicago blues thrived as well, and I was there to soak it all up. I loved listening to the diverse styles of the blues performers—the powerhouse delivery of Valerie Wellington, the jaw-dropping guitar work of Melvin Taylor or the intermingling blues and reggae strains of the Kinsey Report. Wide-eyed and amazed, I absorbed the stories and living history offered up by artists who had lived through Jim Crow, the Depression, the Great Migration and all the joys and struggles that inform blues music. I didn't know it at the time, but these were history lessons that would serve me well.

When I was invited to write the monthly blues column "Sweet Home" for the *Illinois Entertainer* in 2009, I knew that I'd get to delve deeper into the genre I loved, but I had no idea what an impact it would have on me. Interviewing artists and listening to new blues albums every month reconnected me to the Chicago blues scene. I visited the new clubs and discovered new artists and the new millennium challenges they faced trying to keep the blues invigorated. Soon, I was regularly giving Chicago visitors the inside scoop on blues people and places they couldn't miss. This book is an extension of that information. It represents the Chicago blues history and experiences I've gleaned over the years that I believe are important for any blues fan or Chicago visitor to witness. It also represents my heritage and the love I have for this happy, raunchy, melancholy music that forms the foundation for all American popular music, from soul to jazz to rock. Chicago blues is music and also a culture that I'm excited to show you.

PART I
CHICAGO BLUES HISTORY

I

From Mississippi to the Windy City

The Great Migration and the Blues

The roots of Chicago blues music don't actually start with a particular song or musician. The beginnings of this highly emotional art form can be traced to the imposing mechanical presence of a train. The Illinois Central Railroad, dubbed "the IC" by Chicago residents, transported the blues to Chicago in the form of Mississippi migrants who carried their musical traditions with them. Thousands hopped onto these trains, the most famous of which was the Panama Limited, that supplied service between Chicago, St. Louis and New Orleans. The passengers included sharecroppers, field hands, carpenters and masons searching for the expanse of northern opportunities that would bring them freedom and equality. They braved twelve- to twenty-four-hour journeys in what would be called the Great Migration.

This migration of African Americans from the South to the North helped develop what would become known as Chicago blues. Starting around the beginning of World War I, masses of southern blacks moved north to escape brutal Jim Crow laws and ravaged cotton crops. They migrated to big northern cities to seek the promise of more economic opportunities and an existence free from lynchings and the inequality of Jim Crow laws. The war in Europe halted the European immigration that had supplied labor for northern factories, so northern businessmen eagerly recruited black workers from the South. These were the circumstances that drew hordes of Mississippians to Chicago during the beginning of the Great Migration, filling the South and West Sides of the city and laying the foundation for the creation of Chicago blues.

A stone left behind from the Illinois Central Railroad. *Author's collection.*

"The blues may have started in the South but it developed into a sophisticated art form in Northern cities," explains Sterling D. Plumpp, poet laureate of Chicago blues and professor emeritus at the University of Illinois–Chicago. Plumpp participated in the later half of the Great Migration, catching the IC from Mississippi to Chicago in 1961. Landing in the bustling West Side neighborhood of Lawndale and, later, the South Side enclave of Woodlawn, Plumpp walked to popular neighborhood joints to catch Muddy Waters, Howlin' Wolf and Lightnin' Hopkins playing to small crowds of regulars. He recognized the blues rhythms that had surrounded him growing up in Mississippi, but they had taken on a smoother, electrified sound in Chicago.

The Mississippi and Chicago connection was a crucial factor in the creation of Chicago blues. The Mississippi Delta blues that musicians played on plantations, in juke joints and at gatherings throughout the South was a blueprint for what would become the Chicago blues. Typically played with acoustic guitar and harmonica, the Delta blues sound traveled to Chicago as migrants from rural Mississippi, where the blues was formed, flooded the city. Although people also came from other southern states, figures show that the majority of African Americans arriving in Chicago during the

Great Migration moved from Mississippi. In Mike Rowe's 1975 exploration of Chicago blues, *Chicago Breakdown*, Mississippi stands out as the most frequent home state for thousands of migrants during the heart of the Great Migration: "from the best estimate, the net intercensal migration to Chicago for the years 1940–1950 was 154,000 and something like one-half of these migrants were born in Mississippi."

THE URBAN BLUES

Chicago represented the most direct route from the Delta to the north on the IC, and by the late 1930s, it was also the place where the most popular blues records were recorded. During the '20s and early '30s, record labels such as Okeh and Paramount organized field trips to the South to record the sparse, rhythmic patterns of the country blues. Sometimes the labels would bring the musicians to Chicago or New York to record, but more typically, they captured the music in its natural setting, among plantations, crumbling shacks and a vicious caste system that fueled the emotional blues laments.

A steady stream of blues musicians settled in Chicago during the beginning of the Great Migration, and they adapted their music to their new environment. The straightforward guitar and harp accompaniment of country blues evolved into piano and guitar tunes, revealing a more urban sophistication. The influences from crowded tenements and fast-paced city living seeped into the music, altering the tone and arrangements. The move away from rural fields, where the mobility of instruments was important, is reflected in the addition of the stationary piano, a popular feature in most city clubs and taverns. By the 1920s, this new blues sound was being recorded by Chicago record labels. "Blues singers came from the agricultural class. They were used to the style they sang in the fields," says Plumpp. "They created the music, the clubs and the scene."

The most significant Chicago "race" record label at the time was Bluebird, run by Lester Melrose, who, according to *Chicago Breakdown*, shaped the recorded Chicago blues sound into a consistent lineup of singer, guitar, piano, bass, drum and an occasional harmonica or sax. Race records were aimed specifically at the new African American market of music fans, eager to hear the new urban blues. Not only was the sound different than the stark shouting of the country singers, but the mood was also different. Big Bill Broonzy, one of the pioneers of the new urban blues, sounded exuberant on his recordings. He transitioned from playing country blues on his acoustic guitar to being backed by his Memphis Five, which supplied an up-tempo sound that mixed popular dance music with blues. By the late '30s, Chicago blues had a distinct sound and mood that reflected the sensibilities of the Great Migration travelers who had settled in the city. Austin Sonnier explains in *A Guide to the Blues: History, Who's Who, Research Sources*:

> *Departing from the ease and subdued temperament of the blues that went before, the emotional level of blues in Chicago in the late 1930s and early 1940s was beginning to pick up. By that time the city's black population had established its own cultural roots, and there began a new feeling of assertion in the music. Different instrumental combinations sprung up. Melodic and rhythm patterns changed, and off beat accents became popular. Vocal acrobatics also added greatly to a new musical excitement. All of these elements generated a strong sense of social cohesion and power among blacks.*

The emotional pain of the blues was quieted with a focus on the lively band rhythms. It was as if the prospect of better opportunities and rest from backbreaking labor seeped out from the music and inspired southern listeners to seek out the northern Promised Land. Of course, the reality of this storied city was much different than the hopeful dreams of southern migrants.

The first stop for musicians landing in Chicago was Maxwell Street. Called "Jew Town" because of the large numbers of Eastern European Jewish vendors who dominated the market with pushcarts, the open-air market was centered on Maxwell and Halsted Streets. A hodgepodge of cheap clothes, used furniture, appliances, produce, handicrafts and street food served as the backdrop for the blues streaming out of the market. Musicians stood on corners, in between sellers' tables—anywhere they could find to draw a crowd. By the '40s, they had started to hook up amplifiers so their blues sound could carry across the crowded market. Playing on Maxwell Street served as an introduction to the Chicago blues scene; before the musicians could win a club gig or a record contract, they'd get their feet wet on Maxwell Street. Many blues musicians traveled from the South specifically to play on Maxwell Street. According to legendary Chicago blues musician Honeyboy Edwards's autobiography, *The World Don't Owe Me Nothing*, "I remember when musicians walked from Memphis, Arkansas, and Mississippi with their guitars on their shoulders because they found out they could make some money on Maxwell Street!"

After establishing a following on Maxwell Street, blues musicians could parlay that into playing in the blues clubs that blanketed the South and West Sides of the city. An array of clubs represented the chance to make more money than the musicians had ever seen on southern plantations and in rural towns. It also presented opportunities to play on stages before appreciative, dancing crowds. The best, most popular clubs were all located in the neighborhood where the recent African American migrants were forced to settle. Called the "black belt" and the "black metropolis," the area was teeming with dilapidated tenements, as well as elegant brownstones and nightclubs. This was where the southern transplants faced the northern brand of segregation and racism. Stretching across a narrow strip of Chicago, the area was also famously called Bronzeville.

2
The Black Belt of Bronzeville

The numbers of African Americans fleeing the South and flooding into Chicago during the Great Migration were unprecedented. According to Isabel Wilkerson in her chronicle of the Great Migration, *The Warmth of Other Suns*, "World War II brought the fastest flow of black people out of the South in history—nearly 1.6 million left during the 1940s, more than any decade before." Bronzeville originally unfolded from Sixteenth Street to Thirty-ninth Street in 1900, forming a long, narrow, belt-like shape. By 1930, the thousands of new arrivals had pushed the area from Sixteenth Street to Sixty-seventh Street. The misery that the overcrowded, overpriced conditions created was observed by Edith Abbott, a researcher at the nearby University of Chicago who studied tenement life in the city in the 1930s. As Wilkerson explains, according to Abbott, "Families lived without light, without heat and sometimes without water…The rents in the South Side Negro districts were conspicuously the highest of all districts visited." If that weren't enough, the migrants were met with the same racism, and sometimes violence, from which they had fled in the South. A notorious riot broke out in 1919 when a black boy swam across the invisible line separating the black side from the white side of the beach. In another infamous Chicago incident in 1951, a black family who dared to leave Bronzeville to move into an apartment in Chicago's Cicero suburb had their furniture and belongings torched and their building firebombed.

These are the factors that helped create Bronzeville, an area of the city where African Americans were segregated and forced to create their own businesses since they weren't welcome downtown. So they opened their own restaurants, grocery stores, doctor's offices and even a large department store, South Center. At night, the main strip of Forty-seventh Street was lit up with nightclubs and lounges, including the Regal Theatre, 708 Club, the Parkway Ballroom, the Boulevard Lounge, the Savoy, Square's and Gerri's Palm Tavern. These were the venues where the southerners played the songs that had helped soothe the pains of southern injustice. Now, the music gave solace in a cold and unfriendly city with its own kind of injustice. Inside these dance halls and bars, which were basically urban juke joints, acoustic strains of country blues evolved into the electric rhythms of what would eventually be dubbed Chicago blues.

Playing Maxwell Street was an easy introduction to the city. It was similar to playing the corners and country stores in rural towns; you just grabbed a spot and started to play. But performing inside a Bronzeville club or lounge was a different story. Typically, new musicians would get their starts by sitting in with the established musicians. Owners would hear them and book them at their clubs, initiating them onto the slippery road to a big-city musician's career. Mike Rowe explains the blues club setup through the experience of legendary Chicago bluesman Homesick James in *Chicago Blues: The City & the Music*:

> *Homesick was working with Horace Henderson's mixed group at Circle Inn, 63rd and Wentworth, and at the inappropriately named Square Deal Club, 230 W. Division Street, with the pianist Jimmy Walker. They played for five or six hours, mostly Blind Boy Fuller and Memphis Minnie numbers, for three dollars each. This was always the pattern, for, with the long-established artists like Big Bill, Tampa Red and Memphis Minnie playing regularly at the bigger clubs, it was very hard for newcomers to break into the scene, although most of the well-known singers were always willing to lend a hand to the young hopefuls from the South.*

This was the environment that spawned the birth of Chicago blues. Crammed into the designated black areas of the South and West Sides, the new arrivals re-created the comforts of their southern homes in Chicago. They brought their barbecue and ham hocks, their church rituals and their music. The simple acoustic guitars and personal laments were altered by the big city and grew into bands with not just guitar and harmonica but also bass guitar, drums, piano and sometimes saxophone. The music was amplified to be heard over the rowdy bar crowds, and the lyrics expanded to encompass broader, urban experiences. And they called it Chicago blues.

3
Chicago Blues Papas

The names and talents of all the musicians who have influenced and helped develop Chicago blues could fill a small library. This section will not attempt to identify all of these musicians. Instead, this small group represents the bluesmen who left a recognizable and unquestionable mark on the genre. These are the names that even the most casual Chicago blues fan should know. In order to understand Chicago blues, it helps to know a little about all of these historic musicians.

BIG BILL BROONZY

A legendary figure whose prolific songwriting and guitar playing helped shape the Chicago blues sound from the 1930s through the late '50s, Big Bill Broonzy was a highly versatile musician with lasting influence. He started out with the acoustic country blues he heard growing up in Arkansas, playing the box fiddle and violin. He didn't learn guitar until arriving in Chicago in 1920, crafting a dexterous finger-picking style that he easily adjusted to the setting and style the situation required. Big Bill played guitar for pivotal Chicago blues artists, including Georgia Tom Dorsey, Tampa Red and Memphis Minnie, but it was his years recording and writing for Chicago's legendary Bluebird Records that would firmly establish his legacy.

Bluebird Records was a Chicago label that recorded the majority of blues artists during the '30s and through the early '50s. Most of these performers didn't have their own backup bands, so Bluebird's owner, Lester Melrose, decided to have these same musicians play on one another's records. The result was the "bluebird beat," which Big Bill helped create by playing guitar on hundreds of records. Characterized by upright bass and trap drums, the bluebird beat was the sound of a newly developed urban blues, which would evolve into the postwar Chicago blues sound. Big Bill didn't just play on the records; he also worked as Melrose's co-manager, organizing recording sessions, scouting talent and writing songs, deepening his impact on this new blues style.

As a man of so many talents, it's hard to narrow Big Bill's most significant legacy, but his songwriting and storytelling skills were unmatched by anyone in his era. The author of at least one hundred original blues songs, he wrote classics like "Key to the Highway," "Unemployment Stomp," "Digging My Potatoes" and his most controversial, "Black, Brown and White," a stinging narrative on racism. His evocative storytelling abilities reached into his personal life, which he treated as an extension of his music. He related accounts and sang songs of growing up in rural Mississippi, the son of slaves. It's only recently that researchers have discovered that neither of these points was true; even his name was made up. He changed and re-created realities that best suited the situation. Toward the end of his life, when folk music became popular as a tool for social change, he reinvented his show and included folk songs, creating a second act in a long and ever-changing career. He paved the way for the next generation of blues performers to adapt to the changing musical landscape. He was a mentor for Muddy Waters and an acknowledged influence on Howlin' Wolf, Eric Clapton and Pete Townsend.

ELMORE JAMES

Known as the "King of the Slide Guitar," Elmore James lived to be only forty-five but managed to leave a huge imprint not only on Chicago blues but also on blues rock. His swooping guitar riffs; distorted, amplified sound; and intense, primal vocals served to cement the electrified Chicago blues aesthetic. He's also generally credited with creating the blues rock genre.

Growing up in Mississippi, Elmore learned to play guitar on a makeshift instrument fashioned from a broomstick and lard can. As a teen, he performed in local juke joints with Robert Johnson, the "King of the Delta Blues," as well as Chicago blues legend Howlin' Wolf. After forming his first band in the late '30s, he toured with another Chicago blues legend, Sonny Boy Williamson II. But it was Robert Johnson who would influence Elmore's music the most, affecting his song choices as well as the way he approached them. It was a Robert Johnson tune that became his first and signature hit: "Dust My Broom." Updating the country blues sound with electrified riffs and emotional wails, the song climbed to the top of the R&B charts in 1951 and remains a Chicago blues classic.

Elmore created his sound by rebuilding his amplifiers for a big, distorted effect. He became a popular live act with his band, the Broomdusters, which included his cousin Homesick James, another Chicago blues legend. He ruled the Chicago blues scene during the 1950s with hits that included "The Sky Is Crying" and "Shake Your Money Maker." He died of a heart attack in 1963, but he was inducted into the Blues Hall of Fame and Rock & Roll Hall of Fame for his distinctive guitar playing. His classic blues songs continue to be popular.

MUDDY WATERS

The quintessential Chicago bluesman and the most famous blues musician the city has produced, Muddy Waters's importance and influence on the genre, as well as on popular music in general, cannot be overstated. As the king of Chicago blues, he helped pioneer and promote the Chicago blues style with a startling mix of showmanship, musical innovation and keen mining of his Delta roots.

Born McKinley Morganfield in a small town near the Mississippi River, he earned the nickname of "Muddy" from playing in puddles as a child. The "Waters" was attached later, as he got older and started performing on the harmonica at local parties and social events. Inspired by the records he heard of master Delta blues musicians, including Blind Lemon Jefferson and Tampa Red, Muddy honed his supercharged singing and playing. He taught himself to play bottleneck guitar as a teen by listening to Son House, Charley Patton and Robert Johnson records. By the time musicologist Alan Lomax recorded young Muddy for the Library of Congress archives in 1941, he had already developed a local reputation for expressive singing and powerful guitar work. Muddy moved to Chicago in 1943 to expand his music career. With the guidance of Big Bill Broonzy and an electric guitar, Muddy galvanized the Chicago blues scene. "He gave 100 percent of what he was doing all of the time," said Eddie Shaw, who played sax for Muddy's band in the '60s. "He was a high-energy type of guy; he played ten to fifteen songs per set. We always played long sets for two, two and half hours."

Borrowing from the Delta blues standards he had absorbed in Mississippi, Muddy adjusted them for an urban setting, pumping them with new textures and tones and amplifying them with his soaring electric guitar riffs. His live performances created a sensation across the city, and his legendary band of Little Walter on harmonica, Jimmy Rogers on second bass, Otis Spann on piano and Elgin Evans on drums established the standard against which all other blues bands would be compared. His first hit record, "I Can't Be Satisfied/I Feel like Going Home," firmly established Muddy as the king of urban blues. Signed to Chicago's seminal Chess Records, Muddy was poised to conquer the music world with the aid of veteran bassist and songwriter Willie Dixon, who began composing and producing songs specifically for Muddy and his band. Throughout the '50s, he produced a string of classic blues hits, including "Mannish Boy," "Got My Mojo Working" and "I'm Your Hoochie-Coochie Man." His hit song "Rollin' Stone," which Muddy had adapted from the Delta standard "Catfish Blues," became so influential that it inspired the name for both the music magazine and the British rock group. When the popularity of urban blues waned in the United States during the late 1950s, Muddy's 1958 tour of England revived interest and made him into an international star. Muddy continued to perform and record until the end of his life, garnering six Grammy awards

In Memory
of

McKinley Morganfield
(MUDDY "MISSISSIPPI" WATERS)

WEDNESDAY, MAY 4, 1983
VISITATION: 7:00 P.M.   FUNERAL: 7:30 P.M.

METROPOLITAN FUNERAL PARLORS, INC.
4445 South King Drive • Chicago, Illinois

REV. C. W. HOPSON, Officiating

Obituary for Muddy Waters. *Courtesy of Deitra Farr.*

and inductions into the Blues Hall of Fame and the Rock & Roll Hall of Fame. His legacy reaches throughout the blues and into rock, touching every electric guitarist and emotional singer who draws on the Delta blues.

JIMMY REED

As the most commercially successful Chicago bluesman of his era, Jimmy Reed introduced his distinctive and accessible blues style to a wide mainstream audience. His garbled and laid-back singing, coupled with simple guitar patterns and easy flowing harmonica, were instantly recognizable on his sizeable number of hits throughout the postwar period of the 1950s and '60s. He topped the R&B charts and crossed over to pop at a time when only a few bluesmen reached higher than the top twenty, let alone crossed over. Jimmy's relaxed style helped widen the influence and visibility of urban blues.

He grew up in Mississippi and learned guitar and harmonica from his friend and Delta master musician Eddie Taylor, who would continue to be Jimmy's musical partner for much of his career. Eddie's rhythmic guitar playing was a hallmark of the Jimmy Reed sound. Jimmy took the expected path to Chicago to build his musical opportunities in 1943 but was drafted into the navy soon after. After serving two years, he returned to the city and performed with Eddie and other Chicago musicians, including a drummer who helped him garner a record deal with Vee Jay. That drummer switched to guitar and vocals and became famous as the blues guitar idol Albert King. Jimmy moved to nearby Gary, Indiana, to work in a meatpacking plant, but he soon earned fame as well. Jimmy's first hit record, "You Don't Have to Go," released in 1955, set the stage for a decade of hits.

Jimmy's affable delivery and breezy guitar shuffles sharply contrasted with the more aggressive style of his peers, helping his sound stand out. His chart-topping tunes, including "Bright Lights, Big City," "Baby What You Want Me to Do" and "Big Boss Man," have become part of the standard blues repertoire, and his influence can be heard in a diverse group of performers, including Slim Harpo, Stevie Wonder, the Rolling Stones and Bob Dylan.

SONNY BOY WILLIAMSON I

The first harmonica player to perform and record in the Chicago blues style, Sonny Boy Williamson I revolutionized blues harp performance, transforming it from a mere side instrument to a lead position in blues bands. A virtuoso musician who quickly advanced the way the harp was played, he inspired generations of harmonica players. Sonny Boy Williamson I is the most significant harmonica player of the prewar blues era. According to Austin Sonnier Jr. in *A Guide to the Blues*:

> *This instrument had always played a part in the blues and jug bands, mostly as an accompaniment. Sonny Boy changed its role. He was a lead man, completely attached to his instrument, and he made the harp (harmonica) a focal point in his music. The interplay between instrumental riffs and voice was innovative, bringing him rapid rise and widespread fame as a bluesman in Chicago.*

Born John Lee Williamson in Tennessee, he acquired the nickname Sonny Boy because he was literally a boy when he started performing throughout the South. He was the original Sonny Boy and is called Sonny Boy Williamson I to differentiate him from Rice Miller, who would adopt the same name. Largely self-taught, Sonny Boy was a seasoned professional by the time he reached his teens. Arriving in Chicago in 1934, his stunning harmonica innovations quickly won him a recording contract with Bluebird Records.

His first song, "Good Morning School Girl," later recorded widely as "Good Morning Little School Girl," filled with easy phrasing, became an immediate hit. His definitive vocal style, created from a speech impediment, highlighted his pioneering harmonica skill. A prolific musician, he played on as many as 120 singles from 1937 to 1947. His classic tunes "Sugar Mama Blues," "Whiskey Headed Woman Blues" and "Blue Bird Blues" would influence blues harpists Billy Boy Arnold, Little Walter, Junior Wells and every other harmonica player who followed them. His life was cut short at thirty-four when he was robbed and stabbed to death, but his influence as one of the greatest blues harpists lives on.

LITTLE WALTER

A musical genius who exploded the possibilities and directions for the blues harp, Little Walter was the undisputed king of postwar blues harmonica. Capitalizing on the inroads made by Sonny Boy Williamson I, Walter attached a microphone to his harp and amplified it, birthing a new sound and technique still used by harmonica players today.

Marion Walter Jacobs was born in Louisiana a French-speaking Creole whose Cajun culture probably contributed to his unique sound. In Honeyboy Edwards's memoir, *The World Don't Owe Me Nothing*, the legendary Delta bluesman describes his good friend's talents as an offshoot of his Louisiana upbringing:

A publicity shot of Little Walter. *Courtesy of the Chicago Public Library Chicago Blues Archives.*

Because he grew up in Louisiana, Walter played harmonica in the Cajun style. That's why it sounds so different than other harmonica players. He had that Cajun sound. He had the sound like those Louisiana boys play accordion—he had that with the harmonica. Nobody could match him. A lot of them could play like him but nobody could master it like him.

Indeed, Walter was playing in the streets and in the clubs of New Orleans, astounding crowds by the time he was twelve. He was still a teen when he landed in Chicago in 1947, but that didn't stop him from commanding crowds at the storied Maxwell Street market and releasing his first record on the Ora Nelle label the same year. A singer, songwriter and guitar player as well as harp master, Walter's dizzying talents allowed him to join Muddy Waters's band and alter the path of blues music. An integral part of Muddy's band, Walter's swirling, instinctive harp lines accented Muddy's vocals in a magical way. In 1951, Walter used an amplified harp for the first time on the game-changing "She Moves Me." The combination of electric guitar, amplified harp and Muddy's powerful vocals made them the most celebrated group in Chicago. But Walter didn't just use the amplifier to increase his harp's volume; he also explored sonic textures and patterns that had never been heard before. He would continue to be the studio harpist for the band, but he forged his solo career with the rollicking 1952 instrumental "Juke." He pumped out chart-topping hits for the rest of the decade, including "Blues with a Feeling," "Sad Hours" and "Tell Me Mama." His seminal 1955 number-one R&B hit "My Babe," on Checkers, a subsidiary of Chess, was written by Willie Dixon and displayed the deep connection between gospel and blues by using the melody of the traditional gospel tune "This Train." Walter earned fourteen top-ten R&B hits and gained more commercial success than any of his blues peers, save for Jimmy Reed.

The breadth of Little Walter's work and influence is staggering; not only did he revolutionize the blues harp, but he also performed session work as a guitarist, wrote and adapted many of his own tunes and toured with his band, The Jukes, across the country. He's the only musician to be inducted into the Rock & Roll Hall of Fame solely for his harmonica performances. As a sideman and soloist, he appeared on approximately one hundred records for Chess, including Muddy Waters's classic "Hoochie-Coochie Man." Little Walter died tragically at thirty-seven from injuries sustained during a street brawl, but his influence continues to be heard in the sounds of blues harpists past and present.

HOWLIN' WOLF

With a heart-stopping voice that lived up to his name, no other blues musician possessed the kind of feral, raw presence of Howlin' Wolf. He was six-foot-three and almost three hundred pounds and played guitar and harp, commanding attention with a ferocious charisma that forever marked anyone who listened to his hypnotic brand of Chicago blues. Howlin' Wolf's powerful voice and animated showmanship made him one of the most influential players of the Chicago blues.

The son of a farmer, Howlin' Wolf was born Chester Arthur Burnett in Mississippi. Most of his early years were spent farming, until his father gifted him with a guitar when he was eighteen. The family moved to a plantation in the Delta, close to where, fortunately for Wolf, the legendary bluesman Charley Patton lived. Wolf learned Patton's guitar and vocal style, and he learned harmonica from Sonny Boy Williamson II, who had married his stepsister. He played sporadically around Mississippi but always returned to farming. The turning point in his career arrived in 1948, when he and his band landed a spot on a West Memphis radio station. The broadcasts were

A publicity shot of Howlin' Wolf. *Courtesy of the Chicago Public Library Chicago Blues Archives.*

so popular that he won a regular show as a deejay for the station. This is when he started using the name "Howlin' Wolf." According to Mike Rowe in his book *Chicago Blues: The City & the Music*, "'Howlin' Wolf' came from Funny Papa Smith's famous record but it was peculiarly appropriate to his fierce singing style, punctuated with falsetto whoops and howls." By 1951, Wolf found himself being courted by two record companies, Modern and Chess. Chess won out, and he headed to Chicago

Wolf's impact on Chicago was immediate. Armed with his own and Willie Dixon–penned hits like "Smokestack Lightning" and "Spoonful," Wolf tore down the house, growling, crawling on the stage and mesmerizing audiences with his booming voice. Producing a slew of hits, including "Little Red Rooster," "Backdoor Man," "Evil" and "Killing Floor," Wolf ruled the Chicago blues scene along with Muddy Waters throughout the 1950s and '60s. "He kept the Chicago blues scene alive," said Eddie Shaw, who was Wolf's bandleader until his death. "A lot of people are playing now because of Wolf." After touring Europe, Wolf's influence spread even more, with the Rolling Stones, Eric Clapton and The Doors paying homage. One of the most distinctive and iconic figures in the blues canon, Howlin' Wolf was inducted into both the Blues and Rock & Roll Halls of Fame.

WILLIE DIXON

Called the "poet laureate of the blues," Willie Dixon wrote, produced or played bass on most of the songs that are considered Chicago blues classics. Penning approximately five hundred songs during his lifetime, Willie was the most notable blues songwriter of the postwar era. In later years, he became the spokesperson and triumphant symbol for exploited blues musicians who fought for unpaid song royalties.

Born in Vicksburg, Mississippi, Willie was destined to become the most multitalented of all the Chicago blues musicians. He established his songwriting career at an early age, writing songs and selling them to local bands in Mississippi. His ear for harmony was developed while singing with the Union Jubilee Singers on a weekly Vicksburg radio show. Willie moved to Chicago in 1936 to pursue a boxing career; he won the Illinois State Golden Gloves Heavyweight Championship. After refusing his draft notice as a conscientious objector, he landed in prison, but on his release, he quickly took up music again. Singing and recording with several groups, he also learned to play a homemade, one-string bass. In 1951, he was hired as the talent scout for Chess Records, where he also played bass for the label's house band, produced and arranged records and wrote songs for most of the artists. He somehow managed to record his own songs as well, but it was as the architect of the postwar Chicago blues sound that Willie became famous. He wrote classics including "Hoochie-Coochie Man" and "I Just Want to Make Love to You" for Muddy Waters; "Spoonful" and "Back Door Man" for Howlin' Wolf; and "My Babe" for Little Walter. He played bass on the first hits for Chuck Berry and Bo Diddley. For the Cobra and Artistic labels, he produced the debut releases for Buddy Guy, Magic Sam and Otis Rush. Basically, Willie touched every classic Chicago blues song of the era in some way or another.

Despite all of these talents, he didn't seem to be gaining much money for his efforts. British acts like Cream, Led Zeppelin and the Yardbirds covered his songs, but he wasn't seeing any profits. According to his widow, Marie Dixon, "Willie always read different papers and magazines. One day, he discovered that the publishing company owned his music. They took 50 percent. A 50/50 contract is the same situation as sharecropping." Standing

A publicity shot of Willie Dixon. *Courtesy of the Chicago Public Library Chicago Blues Archives.*

up for what was right was a hallmark of Willie's personality. He didn't accept a military draft from a country that didn't allow him equality, and he wouldn't accept minimal pay for work he had created. Finally, he filed a claim against Chess's publishing arm and regained the copyright to his vast song catalogue, along with some of the royalties.

After settling several court cases for copyright infringement, Willie formed Willie Dixon's Blues Heaven Foundation in 1984. Housed in the historic Chess Records building, the organization promotes the blues, helps blues musicians with copyright and royalty recovery and offers scholarships and emergency assistance. Willie became the elder statesman for the blues, famously declaring, "Blues are the roots and the other musics are the fruits," explaining the genre's connection to American popular music. Willie continued to perform with his Chicago Blues All-Stars, release solo albums and produce movie soundtracks, including *La Bamba*'s. Inducted into both the Blues and Rock & Roll Halls of Fame, Willie's multifaceted talents are still influencing legions of music fans around the world.

4
Chicago Blues Mamas

Women have played an important role in defining and popularizing the blues from the very beginning. When the genre moved from being played only in the fields and at juke points to traveling vaudeville shows and big-city performances, it was female blues singers who led the way. The very first commercial blues record, "Crazy Blues," was recorded in 1920 by a woman, Mamie Smith, who kicked off the classic blues period. The era was dominated by larger-than-life blues women like Ma Rainey, Bessie Smith, Ida Cox and Bertha "Chippie" Hill. They transformed the country blues that had been played by lone male musicians roaming southern back roads into an urban, sophisticated sound performed with full bands on club and cabaret stages. Dressed in gowns dripping with feathers and beading, these women sang naughty, narrative tunes that appealed to a wide audience. Record labels rushed to record these singers who were presenting a folk tradition that most outside of the African American community had never heard.

Of course, Chicago was at the heart of the blues recording craze, and women from small rural towns flocked to the city to try their luck. Female blues singers ruled the entire decade of the 1920s until the Great Depression hit and the clubs, cabarets and many record companies closed. The blues returned to its country roots, and women have yet to gain the kind of visibility and acclaim that they earned during the classic blues period. This list represents blues women who lived or recorded in Chicago and left a lasting mark on the music during the classic period and beyond.

Blues women on the cover of the *Chicago Blues Annual*, 1991. *Courtesy of Deitra Farr.*

ALBERTA HUNTER

A legendary singer and songwriter who started performing in Chicago clubs and sporting houses (gambling and prostitution joints) at twelve years old, Alberta Hunter was one of the few classic blues singers who was able to construct a stunning six-decade career that stretched into theater, jazz and popular standards.

Born in Memphis, Alberta reportedly ran away from home to perform in well-paying Chicago clubs around 1911. Only twelve, she took down the braids in her hair and wore a dress to appear older, winning a singing spot in a small South Side dive. She worked her way up into the better-paying bawdy houses, earning a steady gig and learning a varied repertoire of classic blues standards like "Handy Man" and pop standards like "My Melancholy Baby." After a few years, Alberta's brilliant phrasing and saucy stage presence earned her shows in a string of popular South Side clubs like the Elite Café and De Luxe Café. By 1917, Alberta had reached the pinnacle of the Chicago blues scene, regularly headlining at the storied Dreamland Café. The Dreamland was an elegant club that attracted elite black and white patrons. Here, Alberta became friends with notable performers like the King Oliver Creole Jazz Band, Louis Armstrong and Paul Robeson.

According to Frank C. Taylor and Gerald Cook's *Alberta Hunter: A Celebration in Blues*, Chicago was the undisputed proving ground for blues and jazz musicians. "If you had worked in Chicago and had been recognized there, you were somebody, baby. New York didn't count then," explained Alberta. She did travel to New York to record for Black Swan Records in 1921 and for Paramount Records in 1922. She recorded standards like "Texas Moaner Blues," "Daddy Blues" and the seminal "Downhearted Blues," which Alberta co-wrote. Bessie Smith launched her career as "Empress of the Blues" with the song in 1923. That same year, Alberta recorded the groundbreaking "'Taint Nobody's Biz-ness if I Do," which would become a hit for Billie Holiday and featured the Original Memphis Five, the first all-white band to back a black singer.

Tired of constantly traveling between Chicago and New York and lured by Broadway and increased recording opportunities, Alberta moved to New York in 1923. She promptly landed a part in the Broadway musical *How Come?* and attracted raves for her dynamic singing. She continued her heavy recording schedule, including sessions with jazz greats Louis Armstrong, Eubie Blake and Fletcher Henderson for songs including "Beale Street Blues." In 1927, she headed for Paris and London, where she escaped

American racism and the downturn in the blues market. She conquered Paris and appeared in *Showboat* with Paul Robeson in London in 1928. With the Great Depression affecting most clubs and record labels, Alberta continued to tour Europe, appearing in films and concerts. She returned to the United States in 1937, singing on radio programs and performing for soldiers as a member of the United Service Organization (USO) during World War II. She also made some recordings, including the sassy "You Can't Tell the Difference in the Dark."

By the 1950s, recording and performing options were drying up, so Alberta switched careers. She wiped twelve years from her age, made up a high school diploma and entered nursing school. She worked as an LPN in New York from 1956 to 1977. Forced into mandatory retirement when administrators figured she was seventy but she was actually eighty-two, Alberta kicked off the second phase of her career in 1977. Snagging a smash live performance gig at Greenwich Village's The Cookery, as well as a new recording contract, Alberta collected more acclaim and fans. She introduced a new generation to her bawdy blues tunes, playing Carnegie Hall and the Carter White House and touring Europe and South America. Her classic '20s and '30s music was reissued, and she continued to perform up to within weeks of her death in 1984. Alberta Hunter was a singular talent whose astonishing career reflected the independence and feisty sprit of the classic blues women.

MEMPHIS MINNIE

Called the "Queen of Country Blues," Memphis Minnie was an exception to every rule in the prewar blues world. She was a woman who played country blues at a time when the classic blues women were singing polished, urban blues. She played guitar when few blues women played instruments, and unlike the men, she played standing up. And she recorded dozens of records featuring her skilled blues guitar picking when women were rarely captured on record playing any sort of guitar. A standout talent who played guitar, wrote songs and sang, Memphis Minnie remains one of the most influential blues women of any era.

The oldest of thirteen children, Memphis was born as Lizzie Douglas on a Louisiana farm. She grew up in Mississippi, not far from Memphis, where she would eventually hone her musical skills. A child prodigy, she was gifted a guitar when she was ten and quickly taught herself to play, performing for local parties before she ran away to play for tips in the streets of Memphis. Acquiring the name Memphis Minnie, she established herself in the notoriously rough Beale Street blues scene. She played in jug bands, juke joints and traveling shows before marrying another guitarist, Kansas Joe McCoy. They performed as a duet, interplaying their riffs in an engaging style that attracted a record label. They recorded her first hit, "Bumble Bee Blues," in 1929; Muddy Waters would later cover this as "Honeybee." The song proved so popular that they moved to Chicago to be at the center of the blues scene in the 1930s. Minnie's subsequent guitar showdowns between reigning Chicago blues guitarists Big Bill Broonzy and Tampa Red are legendary. In a ball gown, flashing a gold tooth, Minnie reportedly blew Big Bill literally under the table with her blistering performance of "Me and My Chauffeur Blues." She earned his respect, as well as a position as a major blues star. Minnie also held her own on the rough-and-tumble blues scene. According to Mike Rowe's *Chicago Blues: The City & the Music*, Johnny Shines, a Memphis musician who had relocated to Chicago, recalled Minnie in the wild club atmosphere: "Any men that fool with her she'd go for them right away. She didn't take no foolishness off them. Guitar, pocket-knife, pistol, anything she get her hand on she use it; y'know Memphis Minnie used to be a hell cat."

Minnie and Joe played around the South Side clubs, including Club Delisa and Ruby Lee's Gatewood Tavern, where Minnie's Blue Monday parties were all the rage during the '30s. She broke up with Joe as the spotlight on her guitar and singing skills increased. She toured the South and wrote more blues hits, including "When the Levee Breaks," "Hoodoo Lady" and "I'd Rather See Him Dead." In 1938, she married another guitarist, Ernest "Little Son Joe" Lawlers. They recorded nearly 150 songs together, and she expanded her repertoire, incorporating an electric guitar about a year before Muddy Waters would famously take it up. Poet and writer Langston Hughes wrote about her thunderous amplified sound in 1942, shocked at such loud and newfangled music coming from a woman. Minnie and Little Joe recorded more tunes during the early '50s, but the music industry had shifted from blues to rock, and her health was failing. She and Little Son Joe retired to Memphis, but she would make occasional appearances to encourage young blues women.

Memphis Minnie died in 1973, but her legacy is extensive. Led Zeppelin covered her "When the Levee Breaks" in 1971, and Koko Taylor delivered a roaring take on Minnie's "Black Rat Swing" in 2007. All of Minnie's

A Memphis Minnie record label shot. *Courtesy of the Chicago Public Library Chicago Blues Archives.*

extensive recordings spanning her forty-year career have been reissued. She was included in the first group of inductees for the Blues Hall of Fame, and she continues to inspire female musicians, including Maria Muldaur, Ruthie Foster and Bonnie Raitt, who bought the headstone for Minnie's unmarked grave.

MAMA YANCEY

With a raw and deep-reaching voice that contrasted with her prim appearance, Mama Yancey sang Chicago blues with her husband, Jimmy Yancey, in the 1930s and '40s, but it was after his death that she established herself as an influential classic blues singer. Although she recorded and appeared in public sporadically, Mama Yancey performed purely for enjoyment and self-expression. She was one of the last Chicago blues women of her generation to present the blues in its noncommercialized essence.

She was born Estelle Harris in Cairo, Illinois, but grew up in Chicago. Mama Yancey often talked about her strict father, who didn't allow her to sing or perform in public despite her rich, clear voice. When she married pioneering boogie-woogie pianist Jimmy Yancey in 1917, he, too, looked down on women singing on stage. Perhaps it was a reaction to the flamboyant, sexually liberated, classic blues singers who were so popular at the time that caused the men in her life to have such conservative views, but it didn't seem to discourage Mama. She organized house parties, where she regularly sang a small repertoire of blues standards with Jimmy at the piano. A warm and engaging performer, her phrasing and delivery captured listeners. Mama managed to record songs,

Two generations of Chicago blues women: eighty-something Mama Yancey and twenty-something Deitra Farr. *Courtesy of Deitra Farr.*

including a soulful version of "How Long Blues," with Jimmy in 1943 and, in 1948, appeared with him at Carnegie Hall. Her friend Bertha "Chippie" Hill, an exceptional classic blues singer, also performed on the date, and it seems Mama picked up some of Chippie's straight-ahead, non-fussy style.

When Jimmy died in 1951, Mama began to perform and record more frequently. Often clothed in proper long dresses and pearls, she looked nothing like the bedazzled classic blues singers of her era. Her singing also avoided ostentation; her signature "Make Me a Pallet on Your Floor" packed a gentle wallop and avoided the sexual overtones that other versions emphasized. Mama was demure on the outside, but that didn't hide her strong personality. "She could swear and drink more than any man that I knew. She always carried a bottle of Old Grand Dad in her purse. But she had a warm heart, and it came through in her singing," said Erwin Helfer, a good friend who accompanied her on piano during her later years. She hit her stride during her eighties, earning standing ovations at the University of Chicago Folk Festival, the Chicago Jazz Fest and at club and TV appearances. Her sense of humor would shine through in "Monkey Woman Blues," and her interpretation of Chippie's Hill's "Trouble in Mind" revealed palpable sorrow. She recorded several albums and continued to perform until shortly before her death in 1986. She served as a lasting example of the true meaning and power of the blues. In Jane Bowers's examination of Mama's impact, "I Can Stand More Trouble Than Any Little Woman My Size: Observations on the Meanings of the Blues of Estelle 'Mama' Yancey," Mama explained,

"You got to sing blues from your heart. You don't sing blues from you mind, to go out there and clown for a whole lot of people. Blues is what…comes from your heart."

Lil Green

With sinewy vocals that perfectly accented her clear soprano, Lil Green was one of the most popular blues singers of the 1940s. Her music was filled with sly inflections and a smooth delivery that sold hit after hit. She sang with Big Bill Broonzy at the start of her career and ended with her own orchestra. Although her fame lasted for just over a decade, she carved out an important imprint on Chicago blues. Lil Green helped modernize the urban blues sound and served as a link between postwar blues and what would soon be labeled as rhythm and blues.

Lil Green benefited from a classic blues upbringing. Born in Mississippi, she sang in church and at country juke joints before she moved to Chicago. Arriving with her family in 1929, Lil started singing in Chicago nightclubs as a teen. Soon, she was performing with master blues guitarist Big Bill Broonzy, capturing audiences on the South Side club circuit. Lil quickly snagged a record contract with Bluebird and pumped out a steady stream of hits. "Romance in the Dark" was her first smash; released in 1940, it highlighted her sensuously expressive singing, with Big Bill backing her up with sharp guitar picking. Her next hit was the minor key blues classic "Why Don't You Do Right," which Lil sang with such swaggering assurance that Peggy Lee rushed to cover it the following year, in 1942. Over the next eight years, Lil recorded about fifty distinctive songs, including "My Mellow Man," "Lets Be Friends" and the wry "Knockin' Myself Out." By the mid-'40s, she was touring across the country with her own orchestra.

The changing musical landscape of the 1950s affected Lil's popularity. Urban blues fans preferred the new, more aggressive electric blues, and her sophisticated style of blues singing was becoming outdated. She recorded her last title in 1951 and died of pneumonia in 1954, at only thirty-five years old. Lil Green's stylistic legacy is still visible in Chicago blues; her understated and sensual delivery can be heard in the voices of the many female blues singers who meld influences of R&B with a blues delivery.

ETTA JAMES

An iconic figure who kept female blues singers visible through six decades, Etta James boasted a striking ability to connect with her audience, no matter what tune she sang. With a powerful, soul-grabbing voice that effortlessly tackled blues, soul, rock and pop, Etta James is one of the most influential singers of the last fifty years. A California native, she recorded her classic tunes at Chicago's Chess Records and was the label's sole female blues star during the 1960s.

A difficult childhood provided a big source for the emotional depth of Etta's singing. Born Jamesetta Hawkins to a teenage mother in Los Angeles, she was raised by a series of relatives and foster parents. It was while she was living with her grandparents that Etta discovered her gift for singing. Etta sang in the church choir and became a soloist at five years old, performing with the group on local radio programs. After her foster parents died, she moved to San Francisco with her mother at age twelve and formed a vocal trio that caught the eye of bandleader Johnny Otis in 1954. Etta had written a tune called "Roll with Me Henry," and the musician was impressed enough to get the group a record deal with Modern Records. Johnny switched around Etta's name from Jamesetta to Etta James, and the label renamed her song "The Wallflower." The tune was an R&B hit in 1955, and Etta and her group, The Peaches, followed it up with another hit, "Good Rockin' Daddy." Although she was only a teen, the gutsiness and vigor of Etta's voice leaps out of both records.

The group broke up after its last hit, leaving Etta as the show-stopping solo artist she was meant to be. Etta toured for the rest of the decade, developing an engaging stage presence, as well as her blues-soaked sound. She signed with Chess Records in 1960, and the Chicago label crafted her image as a versatile blues belter who could sing pop and R&B. Her signature tune, "At Last," was her first hit for Chess in 1961, and the emotional power that filled her rich contralto vocals pushed the tune to the top of pop and R&B charts. A stream of hits followed, including "All I Could Do Was Cry," "Tell Mama" and her blues classic, "I'd Rather Go Blind." She even covered classic Chicago blues, putting her own sexy spin on Willie Dixon's "I Just Want to Make Love to You." She continued to record for Chess until the late '70s, when her struggles with drug addiction produced more sporadic recordings. Her vocal ability never wavered, however, and by the '80s, she was performing again and releasing award-winning albums, including 1994's *Mystery Lady: Songs of Billie Holiday*,

Etta's tribute to one of her key influences. The album earned Etta her first Grammy award and spurred her to record steadily. She appeared at blues and jazz festivals around the world and was inducted into the Blues and Rock & Roll Halls of Fame.

Etta garnered six Grammys, including a Lifetime Achievement Award, as well as a star on the Hollywood Walk of Fame. She died of leukemia in 2012, after a lifetime of health and emotional struggles. Her music was her refuge, and she always sang from her soul. Etta's long-running career was a showcase of the evolution and survival of blues music.

KOKO TAYLOR

As the most prominent and critically acclaimed blueswoman of the last half century, Koko Taylor is the undisputed "Queen of the Blues." With a fierce delivery and larger-than-life voice that blew away both male and female challengers, Koko literally kept the blues alive for generations of blues women. Revered in Chicago as blues royalty in a city filled with blues legends, she is known across the globe as the first lady of Chicago blues.

From the moment she stepped foot in Chicago blues clubs in the early 1950s, Koko commanded attention. Sitting in with famous bluesmen, she wowed them with the intensity and power of her voice. It was a voice that drew from the very experiences that established the blues. Born Cora Walton on a farm just outside Memphis, Tennessee, Koko was the youngest daughter of a sharecropper who lived in a shack with no running water or electricity. Called Koko because of her love for chocolate, her mother died when she was young, so she and her five siblings helped their father pick cotton in the blazing fields. According to James Plath in an interview with Koko for *Clockwatch Review*, the experience was very difficult:

> *Now we out there in the hot sun and the sun is comin' down like a hundred degrees, shinin' on us, no shade, no nothin' over us. We're just out there, humped over, pickin' cotton or standing up choppin' cotton with a hoe. It wasn't nothin' easy, it wasn't nothin to rejoice over or be proud of—I can tell you that much. It was hard work and also it was work we didn't get paid for. Because, what we did was, like I say, we was living on this sharecropper's farm, and what we made went to the man that owned the cotton field. And we just worked.*

Koko Taylor publicity photo.
Courtesy of Alligator Records.

When she wasn't working, Koko went to church and sang in the choir, channeling her emotions into the gospel hymns.

Koko acknowledged that her experiences working all day in cotton fields formed a work ethic that pushed her to perform an average of two hundred shows a year. She moved to Chicago after she married her husband, Robert "Pops" Taylor, in 1953. Pops worked in a slaughterhouse, and Koko worked as a maid. On weekends, they visited the South Side and West Side blues clubs, and Koko sat in with some of the leading players of the Chicago blues scene—Magic Sam, Little Walter and Howlin' Wolf. She cultivated a reputation for out-singing anyone on stage, but it wasn't until 1962 that the legendary Chess producer Willie Dixon heard her, declaring he'd never heard a woman sing blues like she did. He took Koko under his wing and offered to produce a record for her. Koko's debut album on Chess was released in 1964, and Willie's "Wang Dang Doodle" climbed the R&B charts the next year. Koko's sizzling take on the partying lyrics and the roaring rhythm helped sell one million copies and make it into her signature song. Her formidable contralto and distinctive growls stick in the memory of every listener.

Koko and Pops quit their day jobs, and Koko started touring all over the region. Chess folded soon after, but Koko gained a contract with the local Alligator Record label and released several more crowd-pleasing tunes in the '70s: "I'm a Woman," her sassy remake of Irma Thomas's "You Can Take My Husband" and "Hey Bartender." In 1988, when her tour bus crashed over a cliff, Koko suffered serious injuries, but Pops never recovered, passing away months later. His last words to her urged her to continue singing the blues, so Koko resumed her reign by 1990. She spread the blues message during the following decades, touring the world and racking up awards—she would collect twenty-nine Blues Music Awards, more than any other artist in the history of the organization, as well as a Grammy and five Grammy nominations. In 2004, she was awarded the National Endowment for the Arts National Heritage Fellowship. Koko often spoke about the power of the blues to uplift and act as a therapeutic outlet. She demonstrated that power with every life-altering performance she gave. She passed away in 2009 at eighty years old. She lives on in the countless blues women for whom she opened doors and the thousands she touched with her timeless music.

5

Chicago Blues Landmarks

The legacy of Chicago blues culture is displayed all over the city, in the buildings, streets and markers of this exciting history. Although Chicago blues is a living, changing entity, history plays a vital role in how the culture developed and where it stands today. You will hear many of these places referenced in classic and contemporary Chicago blues tunes, so it helps to understand how they connect with the scene. Many of the buildings no longer stand or are only empty lots, but each of these landmarks represents a significant chapter in Chicago blues history.

THERESA'S LOUNGE

4801 South Indiana

An iconic blues spot that regularly featured all of the original players of the Chicago blues, Theresa's Lounge was the South Side club that helped define the scene. The motherly figure of Theresa Needham, an apron wrapped around her waist and glasses perched on her nose, created a homelike atmosphere. Regulars sauntered in and lounged around like they were in their living rooms. And in a way, they were. The blues is all about life, and both were on full-color display at Theresa's.

Theresa's Lounge, circa 1970s. *Courtesy of the Chicago Public Library Chicago Blues Archives.*

Called "the hole" by regulars, Theresa's Lounge was housed in the basement of a Bronzeville apartment building. Down the uneven steps, past a chain-link fence that advertised bands and hours, Theresa's unfolded in a tight, dim space. Christmas lights hung from the bar, which was topped with the requisite jars of pigs' feet and pickled eggs. Barstools and tables would fill up quickly, and patrons would settle in, ready to drink and listen to the blues. The lounge was filled with local blues fans, but it was a favorite spot for Chicago blues musicians. "It was my hangout," says harp master Billy Branch, who started visiting the club at the beginning of his career in the early '70s. "The vibe was homey; it was like a juke joint. It was the home base for Junior Wells, but Lefty Dizz, Earl Hooker and all the cats would hang out there. I got my degree from University of Illinois, but I got my PhD from Theresa's and the Checkerboard."

Theresa's opened in 1949, serving what was then a small, close-knit blues community. By the mid-'50s, Chicago had gained official blues capital status, and there were hundreds of local musicians and touring ones who streamed into the lounge. Theresa had earned the nickname "godmother of the blues" with her kind and welcoming nature; she helped the musicians on many levels, from supplying a welcoming haven when most of the city was segregated to loaning them money to replace stolen equipment. Regulars included famous names like Howlin' Wolf, Buddy Guy, Willie Dixon, Muddy Waters and James Cotton. Theresa's was immortalized in lots of songs; Junior Wells focused his 1975 album, *On Tap*, on his Theresa's home. The album cover featured a shot of him behind the bar. Theresa's closed in 1983, when the landlord wouldn't renew the lease. Theresa opened a new spot a few blocks away, but it never captured the same magic as the original, so she closed it in 1986. Theresa Needham passed away in 1992, but the memories of Theresa's Lounge still live on.

CHECKERBOARD LOUNGE

423 East Forty-third Street

The old brick warehouse that served as the headquarters for the Checkerboard Lounge didn't look like a place to hear music. A true definition of the phrase "hole in the wall," the building entrance was painted with a rough checkerboard design accented with a hand-drawn martini glass and guitar. The words "Home of the Blues" over the door were the only indication that perhaps this was a place to enjoy live rhythms. When blues guitar king Buddy Guy and his partner, L.C. Thurman, opened the Checkerboard in 1972, they figured it would serve as another Bronzeville gathering place for blues musicians and fans. Little did they know, it would be that and so much more.

An open space filled with long, cafeteria-like tables and columns in the center, the Checkerboard didn't resemble any other South Side bar or lounge. However, the laid-back and welcoming vibe was the same, and people from all over the city flocked to the club to hear live blues by the best Chicago players. Buddy jammed on stage with Muddy Waters, Junior Wells, Howlin' Wolf, Magic Slim, James Cotton, Lefty Dizz and Carey Bell, to name a few local greats. Before long, visiting legends started showing up to join in. B.B. King, Chuck Berry, Stevie Ray Vaughan, Eric Clapton and Robert Plant all dropped by. The most famous visit was probably when the Rolling Stones rolled through in 1981. They performed as the backing band for Muddy Waters, and Mick sang background for Muddy's anthems "Mannish Boy" and "Hoochie-Coochie Man."

Vintage Chicago bluesmen business cards. *Courtesy of Deitra Farr.*

By the late 1980s, the Checkerboard was one of last surviving historical South Side blues clubs. Tourists from all over the world made pilgrimages to hear the blues in its hallowed space. Buddy sold his interest in the club in 1985, in preparation to open another blues club, Legends. L.C. kept the Checkerboard going until 2003, when the city determined that the crumbling building was unsafe. He opened the New Checkerboard Lounge in 2005, at 5201 South Harper Court, in Hyde Park. But like Theresa, he struggles to recapture the same magic in a new space.

PEPPER'S LOUNGE

503 East Forty-third Street / 1321 South Michigan Street / 2335 South Cottage Grove Street

Thanks to the innovations of owner Johnny Pepper, Pepper's Lounge remained a vital part of the Chicago blues scene from the 1950s through the early '80s Taking on various incarnations and locations, the focus remained on live blues for neighborhood regulars. The first Pepper's Lounge opened in 1956, on the same Bronzeville block as the other landmark blues clubs

Theresa's and the 708 Club. And all the musicians made their way to Pepper's Lounge in a network, where they'd stop at several clubs a night. Johnny moved to a slighter bigger space at Thirteenth and Michigan in 1971, calling it simply Pepper's. The shows were a little more elaborate with emcees and a house band. Muddy Water, Magic Sam and Buddy Guy would all play for lively crowds of blues fans.

As the blues scene began to shift in the mid-'70s with the popularity of disco and funk, Johnny changed, too. He opened Pepper's Hideout at Twenty-third and Cottage Grove and featured blues that reflected the times. A young Bobby Rush would perform his brand of blues, laced with a heavy dose of funk rhythm. Harp player Mack Simmons and Detroit Jr. were both part of an eye-catching blues scene that was later documented in the photography book by Michael Abramson, *Light on the South Side*.

As the neighborhood changed and Pepper's Hideout regulars started moving to the suburbs, Johnny closed his last Pepper's blues club in the early '80s. Pepper's remains a fond reference for all the Chicago blues musicians who started out there.

ARTIS' LOUNGE

1249 East Eighty-seventh Street

Few historic blues clubs were located outside of the traditional Bronzeville area, but Artis' was an exception to that rule. Opened long after the heyday of classic Chicago blues clubs in 1982, Artis' was a far South Side institution, drawing hundreds of visitors to its Avalon Park location. Owner Artis Ludd just wanted to open a neighborhood lounge, but the weekly Monday night tenure of harp legend Billy Branch turned the small club into an international blues mecca.

The neat brick building with a yellow sign was unassuming enough, but inside was a whole different thing. A circular bar dominated the mirror-covered room, with patrons directed to seats around the bar by the bartender. Performers were never more than two feet away, the better for guests to grab the mic and join in singing modern blues classics like Bobby Bland's "Member's Only" or Johnnie Taylor's "Last Two Dollars." Fans poured in from all over the city and the world. On Monday nights, Billy held court with his band, Sons of the Blues, and local and touring musicians streamed in to

Billy Branch and Ronnie Baker Brooks jam at Artis' Lounge. *Courtesy of Rosa Enrico.*

sit in. You never knew who would show up on any given Monday, but there were usually at least eight or ten guest musicians, from guitarists Ronnie Baker Brooks and Vance "Guitar" Kelly to vocalists Sharon Lewis and local legend Mavis Staples. International musicians appeared as well, including Peruvian singer Susana Baca.

Sunday and Monday nights were reserved for live blues, but the rest of the week supplied good doses of soul blues on the jukebox and fun-loving stepper's sets, where locals did line dances to a collection of classic R&B tunes. After thirty years as a neighborhood blues landmark, Artis' Lounge closed in 2012, when the landlord opted not to renew the lease. Artis herself passed away a year later. Billy continues to pay tribute to his second home in his music, and blues fans who were lucky enough to visit will always remember Artis'.

MAXWELL STREET MARKET

Maxwell Street and Halsted to Sixteenth Street

Although the Chicago blues sound developed over time in several places, no one place claims more credit for the music's development than Maxwell Street. This messy, crowded thoroughfare represented the migrant roots of the Chicago blues. Maxwell Street was the gateway for the masses of immigrants who moved to the city in the early 1900s. During the Great Migration, African Americans streamed in from the South, and by the 1920s, when blues started being actively recorded all over Chicago, these southern musicians took their music to this bustling street.

Honeyboy Edwards publicity shot. Honeyboy played with Little Walter on Maxwell Street during the 1940s. *Courtesy of the Chicago Public Library Chicago Blues Archives.*

Located on the city's near West Side, the Maxwell Street area was where immigrants from all over the world, but especially Eastern Europe, settled when they arrived in Chicago in the late 1800s. By 1912, clusters of pushcart vendors had established the Maxwell Street Market, also called "Jew Town" by locals. Open on Sundays, this open-air market featured an array of goods that could be haggled over for cheap prices, a variety of street foods and live music. Big Bill Broonzy and Papa Charlie Jackson were the first blues musicians to play Maxwell Street, amplifying their music to float through the crowds. By the '40s, the market was attracting around fifty thousand visitors, and Chicago bluesmen capitalized on all the potential listeners. Legendary Chicago bluesman Honeyboy Edwards remembered arriving on Maxwell Street in 1945 in *The World Don't Owe Me Nothing*:

> *Musicians come to Chicago from everywhere then just to play on Maxwell Street. Because they could make a living there…Just strung out all hooked up to different people's houses. Musicians would give the people in the*

houses two dollars to plug their instruments up in their houses. And there were so many people in Jewtown you couldn't walk the streets.

The smell of grilled onions slathered on the famous Maxwell Street polish sausages, bargain deals on anything you could think of and the electrified sounds of the Chicago blues were the hallmarks of the Maxwell Street experience. It was immortalized in the 1980 movie *The Blues Brothers* when John Lee Hooker sets the street rocking with his song "Boom, Boom." Urban renewal closed down the market and moved it a few blocks east in 1994. It was moved again to Desplaines and Roosevelt in 2008. The new Maxwell Street is cleaner, safer and smaller than the original; it's also devoid of any spirit or character. The market occasionally features live blues, but the focus is mainly on the food vendors. The sound of Maxwell Street still lives on in the Chicago blues.

ILLINOIS CENTRAL RAILROAD MARKER / MISSISSIPPI BLUES TRAIL

120 East Roosevelt Road

Located on the southern edge of Grant Park, the Chicago marker on the Mississippi blues trail is easy to miss. Positioned directly across from the attention-grabbing "Agora" sculptures of headless iron torsos, the blues sign is overshadowed by the beauty and bustling activity of the park. But from 1893 to 1974, all the activity was centered just across the street from the sign, where the Illinois Central (IC) Railroad station stood. The railroad would stop at the lively station, dropping off hundreds of African Americans who left the South for the North during the Great Migration, spanning from 1915 to 1970. And what has that got to do with the Chicago blues? Everything. This was the spot where thousands of Mississippians arrived, including Muddy Waters, Jimmy Rogers, Howlin' Wolf, Willie Dixon and Elmore James, bringing with them the Delta blues that they would transform into the Chicago blues. It's the spot where their dreams of the storied North were first brought to reality by touching down in the Chicago IC train station.

There are two large stones from the Illinois Central station that remain near the Mississippi Blues Trail marker. Crumbling but with the elaborate script that testifies to its one-time importance, the stones echo the strong

Chicago blues trail marker *Author's collection.*

resolve those new migrants would need to demonstrate in order to survive in the big city. Lean against one of the stones and listen to the rushing traffic and hustling people. Imagine the loneliness, fear and isolation that those early migrants must have felt, and you have the beginnings of what helped create the Chicago blues. The blues has traveled a long way from the Mississippi Delta, both literally and figuratively. The world honors the genre as the ultimate American folk music that birthed all popular American musical forms. The Chicago blues is such an integral part of the genre that the Mississippi Blues Trail includes Chicago as one of only a handful of markers out of the state of Mississippi and only two located in the North.

At the unveiling in 2009, Eddy "the Chief" Clearwater and Eddie C. Campbell shared their experiences arriving on the IC from Mississippi during the dedication. They brought to life the very real emotions and longings that they would eventually pour into the Chicago blues. The Mississippi Blues Trail celebrates the musicians, record label owners, deejays and club owners who helped create the Chicago blues. You can grab maps and apps to visit the marker or the whole trail at the blues trail website: http://msbluestrail. org/blues-trail-markers/chicago.

Chess Records /
Willie Dixon Blues Heaven Foundation

2120 South Michigan Avenue / (312) 808-1286

The recorded history of the postwar Chicago blues is closely entwined with the legendary Chess Records. Founded in 1950 by Polish immigrant brothers Leonard and Phil Chess, the label produced most of the era's seminal blues songs, including Muddy Waters's "Hoochie-Coochie Man," Howlin Wolf's "Backdoor Man," Little Walter's "My Babe" and Etta James's "I'd Rather Go Blind." Chess Records also helped influence the shift of blues into rock 'n' roll with Chuck Berry's "Maybelline" and Bo Diddley's "I'm a Man"

The original Chicago Record Row area was fittingly on Cottage Grove between Forty-seventh and Fiftieth Streets, near the thriving Bronzeville blues lounges. This is where the Chess brothers founded the Aristocrat label in 1947, but by the '50s, record companies had moved to South Michigan Avenue. So the Chess brothers converted an old auto garage on the 2100 block of South Michigan into Chess Studios. The studio engineering was innovative, with adjustable wall panels, a custom-built echo chamber and state-of-the-art microphones. It was here that songwriter, bassist and producer Willie Dixon organized famous recording sessions with the city's biggest blues stars. The studio's address was immortalized by the Rolling Stones with an instrumental tune they recorded at Chess in 1964, as well as their first U.S. hit, "It's All Over Now." Chess moved to a bigger space at 320 East Twenty-first Street in 1965. By the early '70s, Chess Records had ceased to operate as an independent label, but the string of blues, R&B and rock hits that the studio produced remain an important part of American music history.

In 1990, Willie Dixon spearheaded buying the crumbling Chess Records building and getting it declared a Chicago landmark. After renovations, the historical location became the headquarters for the Willie Dixon Blues Heaven Foundation. The organization provides scholarships and royalty recovery advice for musicians, as well as emergency assistance for musicians. The foundation hosts tours of the Chess Studios, as well as summer blues concerts in the building's courtyard. If you're lucky, your tour guide might be Willie's grandson Keith, who will regale you with stories of Chess Studio's inner workings. Although the foundation is open for most of the week, it's not open every day, so call ahead.

PART II

CHICAGO BLUES NOW

6

We Gonna Pitch a Wang Dang Doodle

Blues Clubs for a Real Blues Experience

In Chicago, you can hear the blues in a lot of places in all sorts of ways. As the famous "home of the blues," the sounds of twelve-bar blues rhythms are as ubiquitous as frosty noses in January. But that doesn't mean all these offerings are good; they're just readily available. There are dozens of official blues clubs and scads of unofficial bars and restaurants that will serve up tourist-ready blues performances, but listed here are my recommendations for places where you will not just hear the blues but also experience it. A true blues experience reaches beyond hearing classic blues tunes. It touches the listener in some personal way. Craft beers, a limited set list of recognizable blues hits and trendy neighborhoods don't make for great blues bars; it's the music and the atmosphere that create this. The essence of the Chicago blues experience is captured with music that connects to the soul and a setting that honors that. Here's where you'll find it.

ROSA'S BLUES LOUNGE

3420 West Armitage Street / (773) 342-0452

On a nondescript stretch on the northwest side of Chicago, Rosa's Lounge beckons with strains of guitars, harps and pianos floating through the streets. Inside, a dim room displays typical blues joint fare—a pool table, elongated

Rosa's Blues Lounge. *Courtesy of Tony Manguillo.*

bar and small tables and chairs scattered over a battered hardwood floor. It looks pretty ordinary save for the wall hangings of vivid figurative art and photos of blues giants who have played at the club that hint at the exceptional nature of Rosa's. A family-run bar that bills itself as "Chicago's Friendliest Blues Lounge," it's the warmth and genuine love of the blues seeping into every corner that makes Rosa's stand out. Many blues clubs will feature performers known as gimmicky crowd pleasers, with just a passing consideration to the quality and creative integrity of the music. You won't find any gimmicks at Rosa's. What you will find is an eclectic mix of performers who offer lively demonstrations of the sprawling blues genre. You'll hear famous Grammy-winning artists, obscure singers rarely heard outside their region and popular local musicians, all keenly displaying some aspect of the blues tradition.

But the music is only half of the equation. The other half falls under the gregarious charm of owner Tony Manguillo and his mother, Rosa. In a story that sounds like a trumped-up blues narrative, Tony grew up loving the blues in a small town outside Milan, Italy. He played drums in a local blues band, and when legendary harpist Junior Wells toured Italy, he caught his show and shared a bottle of J&B with the Chicago bluesman. Junior gave

Tony his address and told him to look him up if he ever came to Chicago. Chasing his dream to play Chicago blues, Tony did just that, landing at the celebrated blues club Theresa's Lounge. Impressed by how the people at Theresa's quickly took him in and made him feel at home, he modeled his own club after it. He named it for his mother, a silver-haired matriarch who quickly followed him to Chicago to make sure he was all right. Rosa's is the type of place where neighborhood regulars, serious blues fans and casual onlookers all feel comfortable hanging out.

Most nights, Tony himself will welcome you with a hearty greeting dipped in his heavy Italian accent and a pat on the back. Mama Rosa serves up drinks at the bar or sometimes crushes opponents in fierce pool games. Grab a seat at the bar or a table in front; the shows are always engaging and off the cuff. Regulars include virtuoso blues guitarist and member of the extended Rosa's family Melvin Taylor, noted Chicago bluesman James Wheeler and master blues harpists Billy Branch and Sugar Blue.

BUDDY GUY'S LEGENDS

700 South Wabash Street / (312) 427-1190

With an iconic bluesman as the owner, Buddy Guy's Legends draws blues fans from all over the world. Located behind two hotels in the South Loop neighborhood of downtown, you would expect the club to be constantly filled with big-eyed tourists—and it is. However, this doesn't take away from the fact that Legends supplies some of the best live blues performances in the city and the country as a whole. The layout is spacious, with two levels and dozens of chairs and tables, but the place is usually packed to capacity so this point is barely noticeable. A full-service kitchen dishing up Buddy's native Louisiana cuisine helps lend the space more intimacy, with the gumbo and fried okra conjuring images of late-night juke joint parties. The décor illustrates the distinction of Buddy's career, with Grammys, a Rock & Roll Hall of Fame statue and an assortment of signed guitars, including instruments from B.B. King, Carlos Santana and Stevie Ray Vaughn. Compared to the relaxed layout of typical blues clubs, the seating setup is a little different at Legends. Although you can buy tickets at the door, most national acts sell out in advance, and seating is first come, first serve, no matter how far in advance you buy your tickets. What this means

Interior of Legends, with a painting of Buddy Guy flanked by his guitars. *Author's collection.*

is that if you don't buy your ticket in advance and arrive at least two hours before the music starts, you will be standing the entire night, which is best spent dancing. Each night starts out with an acoustic set that showcases local talent before the opening and headline acts. Legends is open to all ages for lunch and free acoustic sets until 8:00 p.m., when it turns into a twenty-one-and-over club.

The popular appeal of Legends is directly related to the star power of Buddy Guy. Unlike some celebrity nightclubs and restaurants, Buddy doesn't just lend his name to the place; he actually hangs out there. Besides his famous January residence, when he plays sold-out shows at Legends all month, you can catch Buddy at the bar, or if you're lucky, he'll do an impromptu song with a featured artist. The most famous living legend of the Chicago blues, Buddy moved to Chicago from Louisiana just as the Chicago blues was gaining worldwide visibility in the late 1950s. He honed his jaw-dropping guitar magic working as a sideman behind blues greats like Muddy Waters, Howlin' Wolf and Koko Taylor, and he opened his first blues club, the legendary Checkerboard Lounge, in 1972. As one of the last historic blues clubs open in the 1970s and '80s, the Checkerboard was a required stop for visiting blues and rock stars.

Legends continues the Checkerboard tradition of featuring blues and rock superstars. Eric Clapton famously played for three sold-out shows in 1994, and the Rolling Stones, Dr. John, David Bowie, Albert Collins and Junior Wells have also appeared. Expect to see high-energy performances that will drive you to the small dance floor in front of the stage. Regulars include veteran Chicago blues musicians like Linsey Alexander, Michael Coleman, Fruteland Jackson and Mary Lane.

LEE'S UNLEADED BLUES

7401 South South Chicago Avenue / (773) 493-3477

During the heyday of the Chicago blues scene, the South Side was a dazzling mecca for blues fans, with clubs lining both sides of major streets and music lasting for almost twenty-four hours straight. Today, only a few clubs remain, and Lee's Unleaded is the most consistent. In an easy-to-miss spot across from an auto wrecker, a brick building perched on a corner houses this blues mainstay. Calling itself "Chicago's Favorite Juke Joint," the atmosphere in Lee's Unleaded is old school and unpretentious.

The doorman warmly greets you as you enter this throwback to another era. Mirrors line the wall, and the rectangular bar rises above plush crimson carpeting. The shadowy room is narrow, with a smattering of tables and chairs as well as padded vinyl bar stools. The crowd is a mix of neighborhood regulars, classic blues fans and a few University of Chicago students. A neighborhood institution since the early 1970s, when it was called Queen Bee's, the space has claimed several different owners but hasn't changed much over the decades. The vibe is authentic blues bar, with the waitresses calling every patron "baby" and the stage a shoebox-sized platform within whispering distance from the tables.

Lee's stays true to the classic theme with a musical lineup that reflects straight-ahead Chicago blues. Shows are only on the weekend and feature Chicago blues mainstays like blues diva Katherine Davis, flashy blues crooner Shorty Mack and soul-belting newcomer Mz. Peaches.

LINDA'S PLACE

1044 West Fifty-first Street / (773)373-2351

Another South Side holdover, Linda's Place bestows visitors with the feeling that they've entered a neighborhood house party presided over by ingratiating hosts. Surrounded by vacant lots and crumbling buildings, Linda's Place, also called Linda's Lounge, offers a festive and communal spirit to an area that really needs it. A glowing Miller High Life sign over the first-floor window of a two-flat building is the only indication that this place might offer something different than the surrounding structures. A closer look will reveal "Linda's Place" in white letters underneath the window's black iron bars. Stepping past the sign and inside the bar reveals a whole different world of music and hospitality. Considering its association with passion and boldness, red is a very blues-friendly color. It's a hue that appears in the décor of many blues clubs, but Linda's makes it an eye-popping focal point with a long red bar, shiny red cocktail tables and red vinyl stools. Hanging glass lights intensify the bright effect—there's no hiding under dim lights and shadows at Linda's.

Linda herself will welcome you with a hug. Linda's Place really is an extension of her warm personality, and the hominess of the space is everywhere, from the photos of regulars taped to the mirror to the regulars playing pool with gusto. The crowd is mostly middle-aged neighborhood folks who come to laugh, drink and listen to the kind of live blues that you'll rarely hear on the North Side of the city; that is, the kind of blues that stems from crowd interaction and the emotional give and take of audience and player. Intimacy is required for this kind of connection, and that's hard to capture in big, crowded spaces. But it happens all the time at Linda's Place.

Although other local blues musicians might drop in, the musical lineup of Linda's Places focuses on Fantastic L-Roy & the Bulletproof Band, emphasis on fantastic. A Mississippi-born bluesman who sways more toward soul blues than classic blues, L-Roy snatches all attention with a flamboyant presence and vocal gymnastics. Armed with a cordless mic, L-Roy roams the room singing a medley of blues and soul hits while simultaneously flirting, talking and, sometimes, pouring a drink. The Bulletproof Band supplies a tight, rhythmic backdrop, shifting with all of L-Roy's musical turns.

Water Hole Lounge

1400 South Western Street / (312)243-7988

The West Side was once as important as the South Side for showcasing the glories of Chicago blues, but the Water Hole Lounge is one of only a few examples of that legacy that are still left. Sitting on a quiet corner near a viaduct, the lounge's unassuming brick building resembles a typical dive bar, with faded window fixtures and a decades-old elevated sign. The interior continues the hole-in-the-wall feel with slate painted walls, twinkling holidays lights hanging along the ceiling and worn vinyl chairs surrounding small tables. A jukebox filled with soul and blues hits and a polished oak bar command most of the spotlight, but the music room in the back of the lounge contains the real action. Owner Tony Anthony, in his trademark fedora, greets visitors with a smile as they flock to his two-decades-old lounge.

Filled with neighborhood regulars seven nights a week, Fridays and Sundays are the days that turn the Water Hole Lounge into the city's liveliest juke joint. An eclectic roster of local, regional and international musicians performs on the small, makeshift stage, and there is always dancing in between the tables, in front of the bar and near the stage. The freewheeling, homespun attitude is amplified by a kitchen that turns out baskets of well-seasoned, deep-fried chicken wings and fries, which usually cover most tables in the bar. There are also homemade pizzas and burgers, but essential soul food dishes like ham and greens and, on New Year's Eve, black-eyed peas and cornbread mark the Water Hole as a comfortable blues spot.

The music schedule also includes jazz and soul on the last Friday of every month, but the lounge emphasizes live blues on Fridays and Sundays. Blues musicians come from all over to play at the Water Hole, but watch for standout locals like Toronzo Cannon and twenty-something blues vocalist Brother Jacob.

Blue Chicago

536 North Clark Street / (312) 661-0100

Most of the popular tourist-trap blues clubs that blanket the North Side are missing here for a good reason. It's very difficult to gain a personal blues experience when the setting is more geared toward external factors like chugging alcohol or presenting blues musicians as circus performers. Although these clubs all feature talented performers, the atmosphere is often limiting for real interactions. Blue Chicago is included here because it's the only club that focuses on female blues singers, who are often overlooked by other clubs and the blues industry as a whole. Although early blues was popularized largely by women like Bessie Smith and Ma Rainey, contemporary blues women often struggle for recognition today. Blue Chicago presents an intimate spotlight for Chicago's powerhouse blues women that makes it worth venturing into this touristy area.

The neon blue sign for Blue Chicago flashes over a corner building with white arched windows. It is not easy to overlook this club, even though it's surrounded by masses of hotels, restaurants and bars. Once you move past Lorenzo, the bouncer, you'll be able to view the entire place in one glance. Tiny and narrow, you can walk the whole space in a few minutes. A red fluorescent Capitol Records sign glows above the bar and over a wall plastered with foreign currency from the assortment of international tourists who flock to the club. An oriental rug covers the postage stamp–sized stage, and a smattering of barstools and tables line the floor. The walls feature framed paintings of blues scenes by artist John Carroll Doyle, and the bathrooms are adorned with graffiti and saucy advice. The opening act is usually a band that plays blues and R&B as the club fills up for the headliner. Arriving an hour before the scheduled show is a good idea because the place is truly tight, and seats run out fast. You'll be rubbing elbows and knees with strangers squeezing in at the last minute, but that's part of the fun.

The music is consistently polished and upbeat. The owner, Gino, selects some of the best female singers in the city, so the show is always engaging, with a mix of blues originals and covers. Look for veteran Chicago blues divas like Peaches Staten, Shirley Johnson and Nellie "Tiger" Travis.

CHICAGO BLUES FESTIVAL

Grant Park at Jackson Boulevard and Columbus Drive

The annual Chicago Blues Festival, which kicks off on the first weekend in June every year, provides opportunities to experience different kinds of blues styles, all in one place. It can be a heady experience; one minute you might

Peaches Staten and Mike Wheeler laugh and sing at the Chicago Blues Fest. *Author's collection.*

be listening to a zydeco band serving up hot accordion rhythms, and the next minute might find you dancing in the grass to boogie-woogie piano. The Chicago Blues Festival is the largest free blues festival in the world, which means that hordes of people fill Grant Park for each of the three days, typically 500,000 over the course of the fest. Each year, the festival displays a theme that connects to the types of artists and discussions featured. There are four different stages that present different musicians every hour. Local food vendors selling Chicago delicacies like deep-dish pizza and Chicago-style hot dogs also add to the mix, along with music and souvenir hawkers. It's a lot to take in, to say the least. But there is a science to enjoying music at the Chicago blues fest. Here are some tips:

Plan Your Day Around the Music You Want to Hear

Festivals are supposed to be easygoing, unstructured experiences, and that's fine if you just want to listen to the music in general. But if you're interested in hearing specific artists, especially the headliners, you need to do a little planning. First of all, study the program beforehand. The blues festival schedule is always available online at least a month in advance. Go to the city's website at www.cityofchicago.org and find out who will be playing. The artists' bios and descriptions of their music are also on the site. Note the time and day of each artist you want to hear. The stages aren't close together, and crowds can make reaching each one a slow process. Give yourself ten to fifteen minutes to get to each stage. If it's a headliner, especially at the Petrillo Music Shell, you need to arrive at the stage thirty to forty-five minutes in advance if you'd like to be close enough to see the performer.

Each Stage Features Different Types of Performers

Depending on your interests, you might want to camp out at one stage for the whole day, enjoying a front-seat view of all the performers. The Petrillo Music Shell showcases the fest's headliners, and the seating next to the stage doesn't open until about thirty or forty minutes before the show. You can also camp out on the grass behind the shell, but views won't be that great. The Pepsi Front Porch Stage features local Chicago artists, including talented kids from the Chicago "Blues in the School" program. The Mississippi Juke Joint Stage is a personal favorite because it highlights acts from Mississippi

Crowds always dance at the Chicago Blues Festival. *Author's collection.*

or performers who honor the Delta blues style. This is also the stage that presents panel discussions on various blues topics. The Bud Light Crossroads stage displays a mix of national acts with acclaimed Chicago musicians. Study the park map, located in the festival's program, to figure out where to find the stages.

Bring Food and Water Bottles

The festival is free, but the food and drinks are overpriced, and lines are always long, which cuts into your music time. It's fun to sample a slice of deep-dish pizza or a hot dog, but if you're going to be at the festival all day, plan on bringing some snacks or a picnic. Travel-friendly foods like cut-up fruit, sandwiches, bagels and chips make for easy eating. Because of the crowds, anything that's messy or requires space will be hard to manage. There's a lot of jostling and bumping at the fest. Bringing your own alcohol isn't permitted, but a water bottle will save you from the sun that blazes down on Grant Park, as well as the crazy drink prices. Fill up at one of the park's water fountains.

7

Got My Mojo Workin'

Who to See

Chicago is the headquarters for the most accomplished and authentic blues musicians in the world. That doesn't mean that you'll always find them at popular blues clubs and bars. Most of these performers follow hectic tour schedules all over the world and might play Chi-town only a few months of the year. I've compiled a selection of must-see blues artists whom I usually recommend visitors check out. This is by no means an exhaustive list and does not include every Chicago blues musician worth seeing, but these are my picks for artists who deliver the blues in a way that's guaranteed to touch you on some level.

BILLY BRANCH

A charismatic, three-time-Grammy-nominated blues harpist with a staggering Chicago blues pedigree, Billy Branch is sometimes called the "Ambassador to the Blues" for good reason. Mentored by the legendary Willie Dixon and guided by iconic blues harpists Carey Bell, Big Walter Horton and Junior Wells, Billy has dedicated his career to the progress and promotion of classic Chicago blues. "I do feel a sense of responsibility because I was so fortunate to have opportunities to befriend and play with the true legends," he says.

Billy Branch. *Courtesy of Tony Manguillo.*

Backed by his band, Sons of the Blues, Billy spreads the Chicago blues gospel with harp wizardry that melds traditional blues with fresh contemporary elements. A singer, songwriter, producer and harpist, his multifaceted approach creates music that's always grounded in the blues tradition but still manages some unconventional turns, like his rhumba-infused cover of Little Walter's "My Babe," for example. But then, his entire blues career has been unconventional. He lived in Chicago until he was five; Billy grew up in Los Angeles, where he taught himself to play the harmonica at age ten and always carried it with him, copying any melody he heard. "Why would a young black kid play harmonica without any role models? I had never seen or heard anybody play," he says. By the time he hit Chicago to start college, he quickly realized that it was destiny that had spurred him to play. "It was August 30, 1969, and I was seventeen years old at the first Chicago blues fest," he remembers. "It was the first time I had ever heard blues; it changed my life."

His life became focused on blues and absorbing all he could on the Chicago blues scene. He started hanging out at Pepper's, the Checkerboard and Theresa's. "I discovered the blues and the blues was all around," he recalls. Billy graduated, and soon he and his sharply honed harmonica talents were filling in for Carey Bell in Willie Dixon's Chicago Blues All-Stars. While playing with the group for six years, he had achieved "future of the blues" status, playing the Berlin Jazz Festival with Lurrie Bell and Freddie Dixon as Sons of the Blues. After an almost forty-year career, Billy is now an elder statesman of the blues, having played on 150 different albums that stretch out over the blues landscape, including those of Koko Taylor, Honeyboy Edwards, Taj Mahal and Johnny Winter. He spearheaded Chicago's "Blues in the Schools" program, introducing the art form to thousands of young people since 1975. "Having these experiences has helped me understand the importance of the blues and the value of the music," Billy says. "We are dedicated to play this music with integrity and get the blues as much exposure as we can."

EDDY "THE CHIEF" CLEARWATER

Diving into shows with his left-handed guitar riffs and big personality, Eddy's lively mix of West Side blues and early rock, which he calls "rock-a-blues," turns every performance into a party. A towering Chicago blues scene legend noted for wearing a full headdress and duck walking into crowds, Eddy combines a diverse blend of influences for his singular brand of Chicago blues.

Born Edward Harrington in Mississippi, Eddy listened to the blues standards that his family sung all around him. He taught himself to play at age ten and was soon performing in church. When his family moved to Birmingham, Alabama, when he was a teen, Eddy started playing with professional gospel groups, including the Blind Boys of Alabama. In 1950, he joined his uncle in Chicago and kicked off his Chicago blues career as "Guitar Eddy." He continued playing in church with gospel groups at first until West Side blues legend Magic Sam took him under his wing, introducing him to the Chicago blues club scene. Eddy cut his first record, "A-Minor Cha Cha," on his uncle's small label, showcasing his thrilling guitar chops. Before long, his manager dubbed him "Clear Waters" in response to Chicago blues king Muddy Waters. It later became simply Clearwater, and Eddy started recording and touring throughout the 1950s and '60s, opening for Buddy Guy and Junior Wells. After experimenting with early rock, country and gospel, he developed his gumbo of all of these influences, attracting eager fans to his flamboyant shows, where he might wail the blues as well as serve up funky-roots rock riffs.

Eddy was gifted with a full headdress by a fan in the 1970s, and he always wears it at least once during a show, inspiring his nickname, the Chief. A master bluesman, weaned on early Chicago blues, Eddy is one of a rare handful of Mississippi bluesmen still actively playing in Chicago. His energetic performances and gritty guitar work are Chicago blues mainstays.

THE BROOKS FAMILY

The Brooks family blues dynasty, consisting of Chicago blues legend Lonnie Brooks and his sons, Ronnie Baker Brooks and Wayne Baker Brooks, is considered the first family of Chicago blues. Together, they play Chicago blues with wicked, jaw-dropping guitar work and engaging vocals. Individually, Lonnie demonstrates his almost six-decade status as a Chicago blues legend, and Ronnie and Wayne illustrate how strong the gene pool is. Basically, you want to go see anyone with the name Brooks performing in Chicago.

Ronnie Baker Brooks and Lonnie Brooks perform at the Chicago Blues Festival. *Author's collection.*

Lonnie Brooks was born Lee Baker Jr. in Louisiana, and even though he didn't start playing guitar until he was in his twenties and living in Texas, his music reflects strong Louisiana influences and is sometimes called "voodoo blues." He played with zydeco icon Clifton Chenier as Guitar Junior and released a regional hit, "The Crawl," in 1957. He moved to Chicago and played with Sam Cooke's touring band and Jimmy Reed in the late '50s. Discovering that there was already a Guitar Junior in the city, he changed his name to Lonnie Brooks. He also adjusted his sound from the twangy country accents and added touches of soul to his Chicago blues for a riveting effect.

Ronnie Baker Brooks started playing guitar with his dad when he was nine but didn't officially join the Lonnie Brooks Band until he graduated from high school. He played with his father's band, learning monster guitar riffs, until 1998, when he went solo. An engaging performer and a popular guest artist on many Chicago blues albums, Ronnie injects his music with pinches of rock and soul.

The youngest of the Brooks brothers, Wayne opted to take a different route to the blues. Refusing to learn the guitar from his dad or brother, he taught himself to play, practicing up to eighteen hours a day. "I always was different, I always thought differently from a lot of people...I'm a leader, not a follower," he says of his trail blazing. It's paid off with music that

Wayne Baker Brooks plays with Ronnie Baker Brooks at Legends. *Author's collection.*

draws from blues, as well as funk and hip-hop. He worked as his dad's roadie before joining the band in 1990. He also founded his own label, Blues Island, and literally wrote the book on blues, *Blues for Dummies*, which he co-wrote with blues historian Cub Koda in 1998. Watch for Wayne's more laid-back, contemporary blues style.

BUDDY GUY

Buddy Guy at Legends. *Courtesy of Songhay Photography.*

It's a rare treat to catch Buddy Guy live in his own club. A heavy touring schedule keeps him from performing frequently in Chicago, except for his always sold-out January residences at Legends. However, he's known for popping on stage with other artists at his club. Whether it's a quick guest appearance or a full-on concert, watching Buddy Guy play the Chicago blues means you've been granted an audience with blues royalty.

The trailblazing guitar deity known as George "Buddy" Guy has influenced generations of guitarists with his fiery riffs and showboating style. Born in Louisiana, Buddy was influenced by the sounds of T-Bone Walker and the theatrics of Guitar Slim. He played for a year in Baton Rouge before moving to Chicago in 1958. He made a name for himself on the blues club circuit with his explosive fretwork and showmanship, which often involved walking the length of bar tops. He won a Chess Records contract and quickly absorbed the Chicago blues sound, playing on sessions with Muddy Waters, Howlin' Wolf, Little Walter and Koko Taylor. Buddy's own music, which featured a lot of distortion, was considered too flashy by Leonard Chess. He still managed to influence Jimi Hendrix, Eric Clapton and the Rolling Stones with his progressive sound. But he proved to be a standout on the local Chicago scene, releasing seminal albums with Junior Wells and becoming co-owner of the legendary Checkerboard blues lounge.

By the 1990s, Buddy's rarefied status as the reigning king of Chicago blues guitar was sealed. He earned six Grammys, twenty-three Blues Music Awards, inductions in the Blues and Rock & Roll Halls of Fame and a National Medal of the Arts. Billboard awarded him the Century Award for his achievement as the Greatest Living Electric Blues Guitarist. But he's not just a great blues guitarist; he is also the most powerful example of the connection of blues to rock and all its other popular forms. Watching Buddy Guy is like watching an exciting history lesson.

DEITRA FARR

With incredible range and a seamless style that melds soul and gospel with blues, Deitra Farr commands attention from the very first note. Her smooth and controlled voice tackles everything from raucous blues stomps to moody ballads with ease. Noted for her versatility, Deitra escorts listeners through all the blues variations and influences. "I sing what I feel," she says. "I feel blues. I feel soul. That's the best way I can express myself."

Weaned on 1960s and '70s top 40 hits, as well as her father's blues collection, Deitra demonstrated musical talent early on, performing as the lead singer in her uncle's R&B

Deitra Farr with Junior Wells. *Courtesy of Deitra Farr.*

band when she was seventeen. By the time she was eighteen, she was singing on a top 100 R&B hit, "You Won't Support Me," with a college classmate's band. A few years later, she jumped fully into the Chicago blues scene, playing local clubs and hobnobbing with legends. For several years, Deitra was the lead singer for the blues combo Mississippi Heat, touring and recording two albums with the group. She left to focus on her solo career and honed her songwriting skills with richly nuanced albums of her own. A staunch supporter of the global blues community, she also writes the monthly "Artist to Artist" column for *Living Blues* magazine.

When she's not touring, her local shows often serve as family gatherings for Chicago blues musicians. Look for fellow artists sitting in or singing background to her evocative vocals and trademark smooth blues. "I'm inspired by what I hear, what I'm going through and what I read," she explains of her process. "Sometimes the music gets to me first, and I'll hear chords in my head." Luckily, we get to witness those chords evolve into beautifully nuanced live music.

SUGAR BLUE

A Grammy-winning blues harpist famous for his iconic blasts on the Rolling Stones classic tune "Miss You," Sugar plays an exciting blend of straight-ahead blues with a few twists thrown in. "I used to think that there's only one hue and that's blue," he says of his allegiance to classic blues. "I sort of pigeonholed myself. I grew up old school," he explains. A prodigy who found himself playing with legends like Memphis Slim, Muddy Waters, Junior Wells and Willie Dixon by the time his was in his twenties, Sugar spent decades pumping out perfectly crafted classic blues tunes until he realized an important lesson. "Blues is the root and all the rest is the fruit, as Willie Dixon said so well. This is the time that I've decided to deal with the fruits. I've come to the place where I'll dare to do anything," he says.

Sugar Blue. *Courtesy of Tony Manguillo.*

Anything might include New Orleans funk or jazz licks blended with blues rhythms. Armed with an assortment of harps strapped to his shoulder, there's no telling what tune Sugar might come up with, but you can be certain that it will somehow connect to the blues heritage. Reared by a mother who sang and danced at Harlem's legendary Apollo Theater, Sugar grew up surrounded by luminaries like Billie Holiday and Muddy Waters. After devoting years to studying and playing with harp masters James Cotton, Big Walter Horton, Junior Wells and Carey Bell, Sugar is generally considered one of the most accomplished blues harpists in the world, boasting fluidity, clarity of tone and speed like no other. If you're lucky, you can catch Sugar playing one of his inspired sets with his wife, Ilaria, accompanying the band on bass.

Straddling old school and new school blues, Sugar insists that there's not much difference between the two. "The new millennium bluesman is very much like the old bluesman," he says. "Basically you're talking about how you feel and what's going on around you. A bluesman is a descendant of an African *griot*. He has to take what's important and what's affecting us today and connect it to the future."

GRANA LOUISE

The phenomenon of Grana (pronounced Gra-Nay) Louise performing, her five-octave voice soaring, her commanding stage presence stalking the spotlight as she purrs and belts self-penned and standard tunes, is an unforgettable experience. "I come from a long line of women with backbone," explains Grana of her dynamic attitude. Multitalented, with acting in plays, piano playing and songwriting in her repertoire, Grana represents the twenty-first-century blues woman.

Although she didn't take a direct route to the blues, training in ballet, theater and opera as a child, there were some signs of her future career path while she was growing up in Columbus, Ohio. "My favorite song at three years old was Billie Holiday's 'God Bless the Child,'" she says. "I couldn't even pronounce her name. I'd tell my mother to 'play the pretty lady.'" Singing along to the blues classic, young Grana startled her mother, who tried to figure out where the other voice singing to the record was coming from. "My voice didn't sound like a little girl's voice," she recalls. Indeed, she trained in opera and classical music during her

Grana Louise. *Courtesy of Grana Louise.*

formative years. "I had a seven-octave range as a young girl," she recalls. "I sang show tunes, opera and operettas."

Even though she came from a musical family, with a mother who "had a voice that could make angels weep" and an older brother who taught her how to keep a beat and harmonize, she wasn't clear about what she wanted to do professionally. She acted in plays, danced ballet and sang, but she couldn't choose just one to focus on. "I liked all three the same. I couldn't make a choice," she says. "I had no clue about what I wanted to do. I was doing what I was supposed to do; it wasn't even a choice. I was told, 'You have this talent, you're going to use it.'"

And use it she did. In a career that spans decades and countries, Grana serves up raucous, high-spirited blues in the tradition of great blues women like Bessie Smith and Big Mama Thornton. You will never get any watered-down, going-through-the-motions shows here. Expect explosive, soul-stirring performances that include familiar blues classics, as well as clever interpretations of rock and pop hits made over in a blues style. "I sing real blues. Not rhythm and blues, not contemporary blues, but stone blues," she says. "Blues is performed from the soul, and that's what I always give."

TORONZO CANNON

Toronzo describes his music as "modern blues played by a left-handed Aquarian," but if you don't know what that means, just imagine a sharp-dressed bluesman playing guitar with flash and singing Chicago blues with a fresh perspective. An engaging storyteller and performer, Toronzo supplies the gritty essence of classic blues layered with his own witty take.

Growing up on Chicago's South Side, just blocks away from the iconic Theresa's blues lounge, he absorbed a solid blues foundation by listening to his uncle's blues jams and his grandfather's Little Walter records. He picked up the guitar at twenty-two, observing blues guitar masters on video to

Toronzo Cannon. *Courtesy of Toronzo Cannon.*

hone his craft. With an elegant fedora cocked on his head and his fingers nimbly gliding over his guitar, Toronzo honors the legacy of the blues greats from whom he learned. His shows brim with nasty guitar riffs and gut-stomping chords, but he's also perfected another important bluesman skill: he's an alert observer of life.

"I read, I look, I'm observant," he explains of his standout songwriting. As a Chicago Transit Authority bus driver during the day, Toronzo paints scenes of contemporary Chicago life that few can match. "When I'm on the bus, I take notes at the red light," he says. His keen eyes and ears combine with his emotional awareness to turn snippets of bus scenes, friends, situations and personal experiences into the kind of blues songs you'll want to hear again and again. He's also a social media master. His hilarious Facebook statuses and Bluesman 101 rules keep the blues alive on the web.

PEACHES STATEN

Flaunting a perfect pitch and a dynamic stage presence, Peaches Staten was born to be a blues diva. Gliding around the stage and accenting her raspy lyrics with kicks, she grabs your attention and won't let go. Yet beyond the dazzling showmanship, you can glimpse a humble Mississippi girl who just loves to sing.

Growing up in the Mississippi Delta, Peaches was surrounded by music. Her mother was a singer, and her dad, a drummer. They traveled around the state performing in juke joints and small clubs. Her entire family, save for a few unlucky siblings, play instruments or sing. But it didn't occur to Peaches

Peaches Staten. *Courtesy of Tony Manguillo.*

that she could be a professional singer until long after her family had moved to Chicago. "I watched my mom and dad pick cotton in the hot sun," she says. "We moved to Chicago so that they could make a better living. It was about survival. They stopped performing. My mom said there was no time to play music."

Fortunately, her strong blues pedigree refused to be ignored, and Peaches found herself singing an impromptu song on a blues club stage. Shortly after that, she was invited to join a Chicago blues zydeco band and became the first female performer in the city to play the washboard. Peaches studied the history of zydeco, which is the folk music of Louisiana's French-speaking black people, incorporating it into her blues performance. Equipped with her *froitoir*, the washboard designed specifically for zydeco by king of zydeco Clifton Chenier, Peaches delivers an exciting blend of blues dipped in zydeco and accented with a high-energy performance. "I try to represent for the women, to let them know we can break it down just like a man," she says.

ERIC "GUITAR" DAVIS

If you're comforted by blues stereotypes and tired musical standards, Eric "Guitar" Davis will kick your quaint expectations to the curb and force you to embrace twenty-first-century blues. Wearing his trademark bandana over his shaved head and tattoos flashing on his arms, Eric plays mostly original, rockin' blues tune. He is not your mama's bluesman, and that's just the way he likes it.

"The blues has always been in my heart, my approach is just different," he says. That approach includes an energetic, playful stage presence and riveting guitar skills. Backed by the Troublemakers, Eric offers unexpected performances that meld blues with rock, funk and R&B, topped with lots of fun. Weaned on hip-hop as well as the blues, he represents the new era of the blues. The son of noted drummer Bobby "Top Hat" Davis, a Chicago fixture since the 1950s, Eric had played behind Buddy Guy and filmed a commercial with B.B. King before he was twelve. He tagged along to his father's gigs at Theresa's and the Checkerboard and grabbed a close-up view of Chicago blues greats like Buddy Guy and Lefty Dizz in action. Although he started playing drums at five and was good enough to start playing behind his father by ten, Buddy Guy soon

Eric "Guitar" Davis. *Courtesy of Songhay Photography.*

convinced him of the merits of playing guitar: "When he showed me the chord on his Fender guitar, that was it. I thought it was so easy. I was into the guitar after that."

You can absorb a taste of just how "into the guitar" Eric became at any of his dynamic shows. Whether it's exceptional cover songs or self-penned tracks, he blasts his guitar with emotion and finesse. He might croon an original tune layered with funk, or he might give his own spin to straight-ahead blues—you can never predict what Eric will play. "You have to have fun with the blues," he insists. "Everybody doesn't want to hear just one kind of blues."

Shortly after completing this profile, Eric was found murdered in his car. The heartbreak was compounded not only by the wife and six children he left behind but also by the fact that, at forty-one, he represented the exciting future of Chicago blues. His legacy lives on in his music and his musician children.

SHEMEKIA COPELAND

The daughter of the late Texas blues legend Johnny "Clyde" Copeland, Shemekia inherited her father's explosive musical skill and started winning praise as the next contemporary blues hope when she was still in her teens. Blessed with a voice filled with enough power and poise to inspire a royal title, Shemekia is one of the youngest and most critically acclaimed performers on the Chicago blues scene.

"My main goal in life is to take the blues in a new direction," she says. "I want to see it go further." With a repertoire that features original blues anthems, blues standards and surprising covers by the likes of Joni Mitchell, Shemekia has indeed ushered the genre into a fresh direction. Groomed by her father to dazzle audiences with her voice, she started performing with him at New York's legendary Cotton Club at nine years old and released her debut album at nineteen. Raised in Harlem during the birth of hip-hop, she absorbed the beats and rhymes but preferred listening to classic soul. She also loved to hear her father play his crisp Texas blues. You can hear the influence of all these genres in Shemekia's nuanced vocals, which combine an emcee's swagger with a soul singer's emotion, poured into the blood and guts of the blues. She easily blends the music of three generations to create blues music that's catchy and still rooted enough in tradition to satisfy the most exacting fans.

Her performances are filled with passion and polished showmanship. She fully commits to guiding her audience through the deep-seated heart of the blues. "I do believe that I was destined to be a blues singer, but at first I thought it was crazy to get on stage in front of people," she says. "I thought I'd be a psychiatrist. I wanted to help people." But it wasn't until her father's health started to fail when she was sixteen that she took up the blues torch and became aware of its power: "I realized that this was what I was supposed to do. Now I help people with my music."

EDDIE SHAW

A legendary and revered figure among blues musicians, Eddie Shaw boasts a storied career that includes playing with the most significant names in Chicago blues. One of the few saxophonists to lead a blues band, his fierce playing and cool charisma demonstrate why he's the exception to that rule. Catching an Eddie Shaw show is a rare glimpse into living history. He

Eddie Shaw. *Courtesy of Tony Manguillo.*

learned to play the blues growing up in Mississippi, traveled to Chicago to join Muddy Waters's band and then played in Howlin' Wolf's band before leading his own Eddie Shaw and the Wolf Gang.

"Blues is a feeling, baby," explains Eddie of his lifelong vocation. "Blues tells a complete story of your life." Eddie's extraordinary life plays through every note that blasts through his tenor sax. He honed his chops playing gigs with Ike Turner around Mississippi. As a student at Mississippi Vocational College, he sat in with the band for a Muddy Waters performance, and the master bluesman told him he'd have a place for him in his band if he ever moved to Chicago. Eddie grabbed the opportunity and moved to Chicago just as Chicago blues was establishing visibility around the country in the 1950s. He played with Muddy for two years and then worked with Howlin' Wolf for thirteen years, eventually becoming his bandleader.

It's rare for a Chicago blues band to feature the saxophone, but Eddie has managed to bring his sharp horn lines to many of the top players, including Freddie King, Otis Rush and Magic Sam. "Blues usually consists of guitar and harmonica; maybe I was just lucky getting away with playing the sax in the blues," he says. A skilled songwriter who paints engaging scenes, look out for blazing duets with his guitarist son Vaan, who plays with the Wolf Gang.

LURRIE BELL

A blues prodigy whose talent has increased with age, Lurrie Bell was born into the Chicago blues and has helped it progress into the twenty-first century. The son of legendary blues harpist Cary Bell, Lurrie absorbed all of the music that surrounded him and developed it into his own fascinating interpretation.

Lurrie reportedly picked up his father's guitar and taught himself to play at five. He was soon recording and playing with his famous father, as well as benefitting from a solid blues education. He learned firsthand lessons from Muddy Waters, Sunnyland Slim, Big Walter Horton and his cousin Eddy Clearwater. Lurrie was sent to live with his grandparents in Mississippi and Alabama at seven, and he played in church and learned gospel traditions. By the time he returned to Chicago at seventeen, he had a full-fledged awareness of blues and gospel, which would inform his sound. Lurrie started a band at seventeen. In 1977, he also performed and recorded with Freddie Dixon and Billy Branch as the Sons of the Blues. He capped off his skills sharpening by playing guitar for Koko Taylor's band. By the 1980s, he had also recorded with his dad and garnered acclaim as a guitar virtuoso and a young blues savior.

Lurrie Bell. *Courtesy of Tony Manguillo.*

With genre-defining albums *The Devil Ain't Got No Music* in 2012 and *Blues in My Soul* in 2013 that explored gospel and traditional blues with soul-grabbing passion, Lurrie is still acting as a blues savior. His performances are expressive and straightforward—no flash or theatrics, just pure blues from a true son of the blues.

MELVIN TAYLOR

Melvin Taylor. *Courtesy of Tony Manguillo.*

This versatile blues guitar virtuoso mesmerizes crowds with his high-speed playing and charismatic, marathon shows. A master of contemporary blues who often slips in jazz and rock riffs, Melvin keeps blues fans on their toes with unexpected detours that always wind back to Chicago blues.

Boasting the perfect Chicago blues background of being born in Mississippi but raised in Chicago, Melvin followed the familiar path of many prewar Chicago blues men. He learned to play guitar from his uncle as a child and focused on the instrument from then on. His family couldn't afford to buy him a guitar, so he constructed his own, throwing together fishing rod string, wood, cigar boxes—anything he could find that gave him the right tone. Borrowing his uncle's guitar, Melvin played Maxwell Street with his uncle's band by the time he was eleven, stunning onlookers with his quicksilver talent. Listening to Albert King, Jimi Hendrix, Jimmy Reed and Freddie King records, Melvin taught himself to play a range of guitar styles from slide to finger picking. Legends like Muddy Waters and Bo Diddley would watch him jam on Maxwell Street, and in 1981, another Chicago blues legend, Pinetop Perkins, invited him to join the Legendary Blues Band and tour Europe. At twenty-two, it was a stunning opportunity to work with sixty-something blues icons. The European audience loved Melvin's dazzling guitar skill, and he was quickly booked to play festivals and clubs with his own band. He recorded his first two albums there and, by the late '80s, was opening for icons like B.B. King, Buddy Guy, Santana and George Benson.

An innovative and mercurial performer, Melvin is best experienced live, when he responds to the crowd's energy, weaving magic with his guitar. You're just as likely to hear him play blues classics by Albert King or Stevie Ray Vaughn as you are to hear a genre-blurring Melvin original, like his interpretation of Beethoven's Fifth Symphony. A master musician, Melvin is one of the best contemporary blues guitarists on the Chicago scene.

JIMMY BURNS

The younger brother of Detroit bluesman Eddie "Guitar" Burns, Jimmy Burns draws from a rich blues heritage, which he displays in a nonchalant manner that quietly draws listeners in. An accomplished guitarist and songwriter, Jimmy performs with a style that reflects Delta blues and mixes in contemporary influences.

Jimmy Burns and Sam Goode at Rosa's. *Courtesy of Tony Manguillo.*

Born in Mississippi to sharecropper parents, Jimmy sang in church and taught himself how to play guitar as a child. At age twelve, he moved to Chicago, where he promptly started singing with a gospel group and, later, a doo-wop group with whom he recorded some singles. During the 1960s, he joined Chicago's folk scene, learning to play for intimate crowds in coffeehouses and small clubs. Jimmy formed his own band and released a few soul records in the late '60s, but marriage and six children interrupted his music career. He performed occasionally but focused on his family during the next two decades. He reappeared back on the scene in the '90s, regularly playing blues that captivated crowds with skilled guitar riffs and soul blues phrasing that simmered with emotion.

Jimmy recorded several award-winning albums that supply the repertoire for his engaging live performances. In his signature fedora, he might croon originals. "No Consideration," which pulses with frustration, and "Wild about You Baby," where he coolly translates passion, are highlights for shows that reveal why he's such a popular blues musician.

8

A Spoonful

Soul Food Restaurants with a Blues Vibe

Food is an integral part of blues culture. The community gatherings of the rural juke joints featured food, as well as alcohol and live music. Dinners of fried or barbecued chicken with collard greens, ham hocks and black-eyed peas with cornbread were popular options. Even the most ramshackle juke joints served up fried fish or pigs' feet and greens to accompany all the drinking and dancing. In the urban juke joints of historic Chicago blues lounges, pickled eggs and pigs' feet as bar snacks were typically offered, and orders from a nearby chicken or barbecue shack were part of the nightly ritual. A few of the current blues clubs do supply a menu of southern dishes, but most don't have kitchens—although food is usually supplied for free on birthdays and special occasions. The restaurants listed here provide traditional soul food with a friendly and homey atmosphere. Drop in on one of these dining spots before enjoying a night of Chicago blues for the full blues experience.

PEARL'S PLACE

3901 South Michigan Street / (773) 285-1700

A historic Bronzeville restaurant for over thirty years, Pearl's Place is a significant holdout for classic soul food restaurants that have been disappearing all over the city. Located in the same neighborhood that once housed the legendary blues clubs of the 1950s and '60s, Pearl's Place presents a tasty musical history connection.

On a quiet street next to a motel, the deep green awnings beckon you into Pearl's Place. With "down home Southern cooking" as its motto, the Pearl's dining room is outfitted with white tablecloths, fresh flowers and carpeted floors. It's a tad more formal than Chicago's other soul food spots (with prices to match); there's even a dress code that bans plain white T-shirts and encourages more pulled-together outfits. Don't let that deter you, though; the vibe is otherwise friendly and accepting. The lemon yellow walls display photos of historic Bronzeville in the 1940s and '50s in addition to records and album covers from jazz and R&B greats.

Diners are typically an eclectic mix of locals and tourists, plying themselves with mounds of expertly prepared food. There's an extensive menu of classics like fried chicken, smothered short ribs, jambalaya, barbecued baby back ribs and catfish. Pearl's is also one of the few soul food places that still serves chitterlings. The expected sides of dressing, mac 'n' cheese, collard greens, candied yams and red beans and rice are also highlights. Complimentary biscuits melt in your mouth, but the best deals are the buffets available for breakfast, lunch and dinner. Servers dish up your choices at the buffet table, but be warned that if you overload your plate, you will be charged for leftovers. Stretchy clothes are advised for Pearl's Place as overeating is inevitable. Avoid the temptation of slipping into the motel next door for a nap and check out the nearby Bronzeville Visitor Information Center, at 3501 South King Drive. If you're interested, call to book the Great Migration and Blues Trail tour at (773) 819-2053 between 11:00 a.m. and 5:00 p.m.

RUBY'S RESTAURANT

3175 West Madison Street / (773) 638-5875

A legendary Chicago soul food institution, famously favored by Dr. Martin Luther King Jr. when he came to Chicago in 1966 for the open housing campaign, Ruby's features the "best biscuits on Earth," as well as a healthy array of value-priced soul food delicacies. Originally called Edna's after the original owner, Edna Stewart, until she passed away in 2010, Ruby's is named for the current owner's mother and remains a classic Chicago soul food restaurant.

Ruby's Restaurant interior. *Author's collection.*

Open for almost fifty years, Ruby's is located on an iffy stretch in the Garfield Park community on the West Side. Walk past the dilapidated buildings and into Ruby's, where you'll be warmly greeted and instructed to sit anywhere in the open, sunny room. Tables and cushioned chairs are scattered around roomy booths that line the walls. A neighborhood hangout, expect to find seniors and local politicians enjoying leisurely meals. (You might even spot a blues diva or two.) The extensive menu, which includes breakfast, lunch and dinner, can be a little overwhelming, so feel free to ask questions. Standouts are the beef short ribs, blackened catfish, salmon croquettes and fried pork chops. Sides of dressing, collard greens, fried okra, mac 'n' cheese and, of course, the heavenly biscuits are a necessity. Be advised that fried items are prepared to order and require thirty minutes. Drinks come when the food is served, so let the waiter know if you'd like them before. Service is slow and languorous, like tupelo honey sliding down a spoon, so sit back and relax a while. Save room for the assortment of eight-layer cakes that will taunt you with homemade goodness on the back counter.

MacArthur's Restaurant

5412 West Madison Street / (773) 261-2316

Another West Side mainstay, MacArthur's has served the Austin neighborhood for fifteen years and boasts the distinction of being President Obama's favorite soul food restaurant. A family-run business that employs locals and makes a point of giving back to the community, MacArthur's provides a good glimpse of the city's lively West Side scene.

If the MacArthur's sizeable red brick building doesn't catch your eye on a bustling Madison Street block, the lines of people spilling outside of it will. The restaurant is constantly busy, especially on weekends. Inside, the wine-colored walls are lined with framed photos of local celebrities, from Kanye West to actor and director Robert Townsend, who have visited MacArthur's. The crowd is usually local families and couples, with a surge of after-church ladies on Sundays. A dining area with maple wood and cushioned booths takes up the center of the room, and on the side, the line forms for the cafeteria-style setup. Stand in line (which moves relatively quickly) until you arrive at the rope that sections off the eye-popping soul food on steam tables. The menu changes daily, but fried or baked chicken is always available. A meal consists of a meat and two sides, but you can always adjust it to your liking. When you step up to the food counter, the server will ask, "What do you want, honey?" Don't be shy about asking what something is out of the twenty-odd dishes displayed. Smothered pork chops, beef short ribs, ham hocks and the Obama-approved turkey legs are favorites. Sides of dressing, mac 'n' cheese, black-eyed peas, yams and collard greens are the popular choices, but you can also choose sweet peas, spaghetti, potato salad or dozens of other picks. Don't miss the banana pudding as you slide your tray toward the cashier. It might feel like you're lugging several pounds of food as you carry your tray to a seat, and you probably are. Expect to take home leftovers.

My Mother's Kitchen

6818 West North Avenue / (773) 887-4368

It's a blues-worthy fact that the namesake mother who cooks all the food at My Mother's Kitchen hails from Natchez, Mississippi, making the cozy

A My Mother's Kitchen hearty meal—turkey wings, dressing, collard greens and candied yams. *Author's collection.*

soul food diner worth a stop for geographic authenticity alone. Besides boasting a talented Delta-native cook, the restaurant supplies heaping doses of hospitality and palate-pleasing home cooking.

This out-of-the-way spot on the western edge of the city in the Galewood community proves worth a short drive. Perched on a busy corner of North Avenue, the small storefront draws in visitors with "Southern comfort food" on the awnings. Step into the dining room and a chalkboard announces the dishes for the day, according to what mother feels like cooking. "Mother" is Carol Simmons, and she bases all the offerings on her own mother's recipes. The standout is the cooked-to-order fried chicken, which supplies lots of crunch with not too much grease. Other entrees include turkey wings, catfish, liver and onions and shrimp Creole. Green beans, black-eyed peas with okra and fried corn are some of the sides available to round out your "meat and three" meal. The service is gracious and measured, with Carol's daughter Kim and other relatives providing the service. My Mother's Kitchen really does feel like you're in the dining room of your favorite southern cook. The coconut/pineapple cake and peach cobbler have been known to bring tears to the eyes of grateful patrons. Like most soul food restaurants, the eatery is packed on Sundays after church, but it's also closed on Mondays and Tuesdays, so plan accordingly.

9

Blues with a Feeling

Suggested Listening

C hicago blues is best experienced live, preferably in a high-spirited atmosphere. The next best thing is listening to a blues album with tunes that conjure up that same spirited vibe. There are tons of blues albums out

Pinetop Perkins playing the piano at Rosa's. *Courtesy of Tony Manguillo.*

there, but these picks represent both classic and contemporary Chicago blues artists who are essential listening for any blues fan. Their albums showcase the rich array of the entire genre, from traditional to contemporary and everywhere in between. So kick off your shoes, pour yourself a cocktail and prepare to get happy listening to some blues.

CHICAGO BLUES: A LIVING HISTORY (RAISIN MUSIC)

A historic, Grammy-nominated, two-disc CD that connects the music of the key creators of the Chicago blues sound with the contemporary artists who are carrying on the tradition today. This package offers a stunning audio timeline of the evolution of the genre, from 1940 to 1991. Music of the most influential postwar Chicago blues musicians, including Muddy Waters, Howlin' Wolf, Little Walter, Magic Sam and Junior Wells, is reinterpreted by four of Chicago's most acclaimed traditional blues artists—Billy Boy Arnold, John Primer, Billy Branch and Lurrie Bell. A thirty-six-page booklet that supplies historical details and photos makes this a must-have CD for any Chicago blues lover.

TROUBLE MAKIN' MAN (YOUNG BLUES)

Eric "Guitar" Davis

A fresh, unexpected take on the blues was Eric Davis's specialty. He mixed hard-driving blues with funk and R&B rhythms for a new school sensibility. This album features all original tracks except for an engaging interpretation of Jimmy Burns's "No Consideration." Standouts include the rollicking title track and "You're Going Down," a mellow ballad with Latin undertones.

NEVER GOING BACK (TELARC)

Shemekia Copeland

Known for her soaring, knockout vocals, Shemekia surprised fans with this nuanced, polished collection of contemporary blues. The opening track, "Sounds Like the Devil," packs a musical and political wallop as a modern blues lament about bogus politicians and preachers, and she channels Etta James on the funky "Dirty Water," but it's the haunting title track, "Never Going Back to Memphis," that illustrates why she's blues royalty.

FIRST CAME MEMPHIS MINNIE (STONY PLAIN MUSIC)

This multifaceted tribute album to pioneering Chicago blues musician Memphis Minnie is a revelation on many levels. Produced by Maria Muldaur, the CD offers new and previously released tunes that showcase Minnie's innovative talents. She recorded over two hundred songs in her career and was the first Chicago musician to record with an electric guitar. Showstoppers include Bonnie Raitt's soulful take on "Ain't Nothin in Ramblin," Ruthie Foster's wry approach to "Keep Your Big Mouth Closed" and, of course, Koko Taylor's seminal cover of "Black Rat Swing."

BLUES IN MY SOUL (DELMARK)

Lurrie Bell

The son of legendary Chicago blues harpist Carey Bell and a contemporary legend in his own right, Lurrie Bell serves up a rousing testament to the relevance and inspirational power of the blues. Laying out the foundation of postwar blues accented with his modern interpretations, he gives a jaunty treatment to T-Bone Walker's "Hey Hey Baby" and flies on Big Bill Broonzy's "I Feel So Good." His soul-grabbing guitar work and evocative vocals throughout the fourteen tracks make this CD crucial to any blues fan.

HOWLIN WOLF/MOANIN' IN THE MOONLIGHT (CHESS)

Howlin' Wolf

Wolf's first and second releases on Chess Records were reissued on one disc so that this compilation is packed with his most memorable hits. "Smokestack Lightning," "Backdoor Man, "Wang Dang Doodle" and "Spoonful" are all here, vividly displaying his menacing charisma. A bonus is lead guitarist Hubert Sumlin's legendary guitar picking, on full display here.

CLASSICS 1940–1941 (CLASSICS R&B)

Lil Green

One of the most arresting and overlooked blues singers in a genre brimming with them, Lil Green defined the Chicago blues sound of the 1940s. Accompanied by the legendary Big Bill Broonzy on most of these twenty tracks, this compilation should be required listening for any blues fan. All of her hits are here, including the sensual "Romance in the Dark"; her wry ode to herb, "Knockin' Myself Out"; and her pioneering "Why Don't You Do Right."

HELLFIRE (ALLIGATOR)

Joe Louis Walker

One of the most exciting blues artists on the scene, Joe Louis Walker always delivers, but this album was a tour de force of explosive blues guitar and passionate vocals. It's also his debut on Chicago's Alligator Records. A standout gathering of tightly crafted tracks, including the searing title tune, the moving "I Won't Do That" and the sly humor of "Black Girls," makes this CD a complete blues package.

AT NEWPORT (CHESS)

Muddy Waters

Since it's not possible to hear Muddy live again, this landmark recording of his performance at the Newport Jazz Festival in 1960 comes close. With a band featuring James Cotton on harp and Otis Spann on piano, Muddy delivers enthralling renditions of "Hoochie-Coochie Man" and Big Bill Broonzy's "Feel So Good." This is the concert that inspired all the British bands to play their takes on the blues.

ON TAP (DELMARK)

Junior Wells

A photo of Buddy Guy, Muddy Waters and Junior Wells, on the Legends wall. *Courtesy of Songhay Photography.*

Leave it to the "Godfather of Chicago Blues" to deliver the ultimate 1970s Chicago blues jam album. Created to showcase Junior's gregarious persona in his Theresa's Lounge home, it transforms Chicago blues standards into his own funky versions. Junior punctuates his originals like "What Momma Told Me" and "The Train I Ride" with his gleaming charisma, while he wrings wailing emotion from his sharp harp blasts on "So Long." This CD is like taking a front seat at Theresa's.

I GOT WHAT IT TAKES (ALLIGATOR)

Koko Taylor

This album represents a treasure-trove of Chicago blues, with Koko sitting firmly on her throne as "Queen of the Blues" while blasting out classics from other Chicago greats. She's in top form on the Willie Dixon title track and her own classic "Voodoo Woman," but it's her cover of Magic Sam's "That's Why I'm Crying" that brings you to your knees to hail the queen.

JOHN THE CONQUER ROOT (DELMARK)

Toronzo Cannon

This is what twenty-first-century Chicago blues sounds like. Songs with quirky storytelling, reverence for traditional blues structure with a modern interpretation pack this CD. Highlights include "I'm Doing Fine," a classic blues lament with a twist; "Shine," a complex blues ballad with three different stories; and the show-stopping title track filled with nasty riffs and masterful storytelling. This ranks as essential Chicago blues listening and not just because I wrote the liner notes.

AT LAST (CHESS)

Etta James

A classic album that display's Etta's famous versatility, as well as her unerring vocal chops. She takes on two Willie Dixon tunes with sexy blues bravado, "I Just Want to Make Love to You" and "Spoonful," but also manages to deliver the soulful pop of "All I Could Do Was Cry" and the title track.

Harp Attack! (Alligator)

This gathering of harp masters remains as groundbreaking as it was in 1990, when it was released. The musical brilliance on display here is unprecedented, with Junior Wells, James Cotton, Cary Bell and Billy Branch blowing out spirited harp notes on eleven classic and original songs. Each harpist supplies a unique tone that complements the others. "Keep Your Hands Out My Pockets" and "New Kid on the Block" are highlights.

Gettin' Kind of Rough (Delmark)

Grana Louise

An exceptional display of bawdy modern-day blues from a woman's perspective, this release showcases a tight offering of engaging originals. From the ribald "Big Dick, M'isipi" to the hilarious "Bang Bang Ba-Bang Bang Bang Bang," Grana's songwriting shines. The last five tunes were recorded live at Blue Chicago, and her renditions of "Back Door Blues" and "Hey Joe" reveal a huge stage presence and vocal range.

10

I Am the Blues

A Day in the Life of a
Chicago Blues Musician

Blues has always kept a' moving.
—Honeyboy Edwards

The life of a Chicago blues musician has changed a lot since the heyday of the Chicago blues scene in the 1950s. The options for recording music, performing and developing a name have expanded since then, but there's also increased competition for entertainment. Potential blues audiences can opt to watch videos of performers online, stream music or wait for annual blues festivals to hear the music instead of hanging out at the local clubs and lounges. How has this affected blues musicians and the blues industry in general? Does twenty-first-century Chicago blues sound the same as it did fifty years ago? How has the profession changed over the decades? Those questions and more are explored with a glimpse into the lives of two Chicago blues mainstays. Blues musicians Deitra Farr and Billy Branch enjoy special positions in the Chicago blues landscape. They had the privilege of meeting and learning from the generation of Delta bluesmen and women who first journeyed to Chicago and created the Chicago blues sound. All but a handful of these legends have passed on, but Deitra and Billy are living connections to their legacy. They now stand as leaders and mentors for the next generation of Chicago blues musicians developing on the scene. The significance of their roles is pivotal as the Chicago blues sound progresses on a global level. Here's a look at a typical day in the life of a Chicago blues woman, Deitra Farr, and bluesman, Billy Branch.

Deitra Farr lives in a cozy apartment in a near North Side neighborhood. When she's not touring the world, she's out supporting fellow blues musicians at local clubs, or reading or updating her Facebook page. As a popular Chicago blues musician for over thirty years, she's developed some strong opinions about the music industry. "Being a good singer is one thing, being an artist is another vibe," she says. "You gotta be able to stand apart some kinda way for people to remember you." With an outgoing personality and a supple voice that effortlessly wraps around blues, soul and gospel, Deitra has never had a problem with people remembering her. She views her job as an individual vocation that doesn't necessarily relate to what everybody else in the industry does. "I don't see the music business as a competition. You do what you do, I do what I do," she insists.

Her morning routine begins at 7:00 or 8:00 a.m., regardless of if she had a show the night before. "I can't sleep all morning. When you've raised kids, you get used to being up in the morning," she explains. Then she drinks two glasses of water, prays and checks her e-mail. "Most of my contacts are overseas; that's seven hours away. I get a lot of messages in the morning." Next, she logs on to Facebook, checks the updates and then calls her dad. In terms of breakfast, she usually eats later in the day. "I'm a brunch person," she says. "I have trouble eating in the morning. I eat closer to eleven." Before she can continue with her routine, she receives a message about her upcoming flight to Siberia. "I asked for a career that would take me all over the world," she declares in an incredulous voice. "When I grew up, Russia was a no-no. I was born in 1957. We were trained that they were our number one enemy. You can't imagine that, one day, you'll be singing there." Deitra pauses and takes in her amazing life's journey. "It's like Michelle Obama, who's also from the South Side, thinking that one day, she'll be first lady. That's a joke! Who would believe something like that?"

The disbelief may have been real at a time when few in Chicago could imagine even a black mayor, but the reality, as Harold Washington's 1983 mayoral election proved, was much bigger than most imaginations. Deitra's life as a Chicago blues woman has reached well beyond her dreams. Growing up in a segregated South Side neighborhood, where few lived lives beyond the mundane, her biggest hope was to someday play music around Chicago. Today, she plays music around the world. "Last year, I performed in fourteen foreign countries," she says matter-of-factly. "I was in Sweden, Serbia, Israel, Croatia, Japan, Brazil, Switzerland, all over. That's a record for me. Usually it's six-seven countries in a year. It's been amazing."

Deitra organizes her schedule around her busy foreign tours. In 2014, the touring starts in Dubai, and then she flies to Siberia. "The organizer from the tour is from Argentina," she says. "He hasn't seen me in twenty years; I met him when I was with Mississippi Heat. He thought of me, and he sent me a message on Facebook about the tour. I'm living my dream," she declares. It won't be the first time she's performed in a dangerously cold climate. Besides having grown up in the brutally frigid and long Chicago winters, she's made the trek to the Arctic region. "I went to the Arctic when I was in Sweden," she recalls. "I have never been so cold in my life. I did two gigs up there, and my suitcase is still suffering. The handle is still frozen up, and it won't go down."

To prepare for her tours, Deitra used to research every country, but she stopped that a few years ago. "I used to look up each country to find out what they're like. But now I like to be surprised. I don't do so much research. I just show up; it's fun to be surprised." She organizes her repertoire of songs she'll perform on the tour in advance. "I send the musicians my music ahead of time," she says. "They have my set list, and a lot of times, we don't have time to rehearse before we leave. I work with the same bands, so they know my songs; they know what we're going to do."

Deitra's typical set list focuses on her original songs. "Artists who do their own songs are promoting their music. When I finish writing my next CD, I'll have more songs to add, and I'll probably remove some others." She also includes covers of classic blues tunes. "I'll do Little Walter, Muddy, Jimmy Reed—you know, Chicago style. That's what my fans want to hear. They come to hear Chicago blues, and I'm representing."

Representing and promoting Chicago blues is a point of pride for Deitra. She realizes the special opportunities that she had to meet the legends of the Chicago blues, and she tries to pass on the knowledge. "I was born in the right place to do what I'm doing," she says.

I'm grateful for being in the right time and place. And for having the right father. If he didn't listen to the blues, I would never have heard it. I came up in the Motown era. They played soul music on the radio. I'd spend the weekend with my dad, and I'd listen to all of his Little Walter records, Muddy records. Those were some good days in Chicago for music. It was a certain vibe in Chicago that's no longer there. It was unbelievable. It was a wonderful time. We had people who could saang. Not sing. The quality of music now is very poor in my opinion. I like artists that stand apart. My closest relatives had strong likes and dislikes musically, and

I was influenced by that. My grandfather listened to country. Old black people raised in the South were exposed to country. My mother listened to soul music from a jazz perspective. My stepmother listened to salsa. My grandmother listened to gospel. I got exposed to a lot of things.

Deitra believes her early musical exposure helped not only her music career but also her outlook in general. "A lot of times, when people are narrow minded, it's because they can't see another way." Listening to the diverse musical preferences of her family is reflected in Deitra's rich musical style. "I had a good background to sing," she says. "When young people ask what they should be doing, I say listen to everything. Little Walter listened to a lot of things, and he brought that element into his blues."

In terms of setting up gigs, Deitra has an unusual approach. "I don't go after gigs. I haven't done that for many years," she says. "I just get up in the morning, check my e-mail and there is usually a gig offer. After so many years, people who want to hire me, they just do. They come to me. I'm visible. I'm on Facebook. I'm on YouTube. I'm in *Living Blues* every month, and I have a website." A strong social media presence seems to be key to Deitra's busy schedule. She books most of her appearances through contacts. "Some people have agents and managers to get gigs and open doors," she says. "I have a lot of musician friends who turn me on to things. They recommend me for stuff. They hire me, and I work a lot; 98 percent of my gigs come from musicians. I don't have a booking agent or manager."

Although Deitra loves performing abroad, she also would like more opportunities to work in the United States. "I wish I worked more in the States," she says. "But you need an agent for most gigs here. I made a decision. I wanted to work around the world—that was more exciting. I got just what I asked for. But part of me also wants to work in the States. I think the reason I don't work in the States is because I don't have an agent. Most of the gigs for festivals and stuff in the States come though agents." Deitra wants to connect with her fans in the United States and often gets requests from fans on Facebook. "There are a lot of blues lovers in America that I don't get to perform for," she says. "A lot of my Facebook friends complain, 'When are you coming to my state? When are you coming to my city? How come you never play out here?' I get that a lot on Facebook, but I don't have the connections."

The way that Chicago blues musicians obtain gigs has changed a lot over the years. The casual network of club owners and promoters has shifted into a more technical focus. "Years ago, you could just sit in with a band and get a gig. I never auditioned," says Deitra. "Now days, you just give somebody a CD to listen to. I also get gigs from my YouTube videos. You don't have to send out anything. That's the twenty-first century; it's different from what I came into when I first started." Deitra believes that these music industry changes don't really benefit the musicians. "They're taping all the shows now. I think its exploitation. People can sit at home, watching your show. Somebody is getting money off that, and it's not the musicians."

According to Deitra, things are also changing when it comes to blues musicians' skills. "It's getting harder finding people who can play the music properly," she says.

> *The people on the scene today didn't grow up with it. They don't have a clue; they haven't listened to the music. I have to ask for eight-bar blues, and they don't know eight-bar blues. They can only play twelve-bar blues. I'll call a standard blues tune, and they don't know it. They haven't studied the music. They haven't done their homework. You have to listen to what went on before you. You have to know your history. The music evolves, but you still have to know the history.*

Reflecting on how some musicians discover blues through other genres, Deitra still believes that they need to go back and trace the history. "A lot of people get exposed to blues in different ways," she admits. "Some find it through rock music. They still need to be able to play some blues standards"

Deitra often appears at local Chicago blues clubs to support her peers, but she rarely works at them herself. "I don't work clubs. They don't pay enough," she insists. "I play festivals because they typically have sponsors. They pay for your airfare, put you up in hotels, and they can afford that I'm too old and have been putting in too many years to be working for nothing. I'm not going to do that. I've paid my dues."

A lot of blues musicians struggle to find well-paying gigs, and many Chicago blues clubs are miserly with musicians' pay scales, which is why so many tour internationally. Deitra doesn't worry much about having an agent and getting bookings because she's done so well on her own. She believes that if somebody is really interested in hiring her, they will contact her. "They hire who they want," she says. "I'm not hard to find. I have a website, I'm visible. You can find me. I'm right in your face."

Being in people's faces, talking to fans, is natural for Deitra. With a warm and friendly personality, she connects with people wherever she goes. "I've got a reputation for knowing everybody," she jokes. But it's true—there are very few people in the blues community she doesn't know. She's generally the first person contacted when a community event is planned, and she spends portions of her day handing out names and numbers to connect people. "One of the things my father always stressed was that you have to know people. I talk to everybody. It's one of the reasons I get the work I do." Another reason is that she's extremely active on Facebook, connecting with lots of promoters and tour organizers. With thousands of friends around the globe, she's constantly posting and communicating online. She acknowledges that Facebook sucks up a lot of her time every day.

"I'm addicted to Facebook, I admit that," she says. "But I use it for what it should be used for, not telling you what I had for breakfast. The good part about it is you don't have to be friends to send people messages. When I'm looking for people to feature in my column for *Living Blues*, I e-mail them on Facebook. You miss out if you don't know what's going on. I'm on there working it the way it's supposed to. I try to stay on top of what's going on, paying attention to things. You can use social media to make contacts and get work." Indeed, Deitra is usually the first to post about blues community updates, including illness, deaths and new shows.

When Deitra is performing a show, she begins the day by conserving her energy. "I get plenty of rest. I don't talk on the phone. I get my energy focused. I try not to do too much. Performing takes a lot of energy," she says. Since most of her shows are in foreign countries, it's a big deal for her audience to witness an actual Chicago blues musician. "Typically, they're excited to see someone from Chicago," she says. "Some will sit there and politely clap. They're being respectful. In countries like France, they don't whoop and holler, but it doesn't mean they're not having a good time." On stage, Deitra prefers low lights. "I like to be able to make eye contact and see my audience. That's important," she says. "I like a cool stage with a good microphone, not too high. I also need a stool because I have arthritis."

In terms of her favorite performance venues, Deitra likes two. "I love playing festivals," she says. "It's a whole lot of people who came to hear the music. There's nothing more exhilarating than one thousand people enjoying your music. I also like the intimacy of clubs because I like to crack jokes. I'll do a club if the pay isn't too insulting."

After a show, Deitra typically connects with her fans. "I usually go sign CDs or take photos with fans. 'I want to come to Chicago' is a common comment," she says. Her after-show rituals involve quieting her mind so that she can rest. "It takes me a long time to calm down after a show," she says. "Your adrenaline is going. I usually only get an hour or two of sleep if

I have to travel. I'm too hyped from the gig." When she arrives back at her hotel, her routine consists of three things. "When I get to my hotel, I check my e-mail, I look at Facebook and then I write." The writing process relaxes her and helps her reflects on the events of her day.

Looking back over her thirty-year career, Deitra revels in the wonderful experiences and opportunities she's had. "The traveling is my favorite part about being a blues musician," she says. "I'm going to places that I could never have dreamed about. I'm going to Siberia. What kind of madness is this? Going to Siberia to sing the blues," she says with a laugh. "I think a lot about my ancestors, the people who came out of slavery and created this music. And we're still doing it, and its being played all over the world. They love it everywhere. I haven't traveled anywhere where people haven't been affected by this music." Considering the popularity that blues has gained around the world, it's ironic how it's taken for granted in Chicago. "I'm annoyed that Chicago doesn't support this music. The clubs are filled with tourists. Chicago people don't appreciate the blues. I try not to get stuck on that," she says with a sigh. "You go where the people want you." Generally, Deitra believes that the blues is more appreciated in other countries. "I think that the blues is more loved outside of the U.S. Everybody knows that way back in the Josephine Baker's days, we heard how they loved black music in Europe," she says. "The people from here, they don't cherish the blues. To be honest, they didn't even pay much attention to it until the British paid attention. A prophet has no honor in his own country."

ON THE OTHER END of the city, Billy Branch lives in a red brick Tudor on the South Side. He and his partner, Rosa, organize their hectic schedules around tours, appearances, shows and family events. Most days bring a flurry of activity where they are answering e-mails, sending out press photos, arranging interviews or writing songs. "On a typical day, I get up and do yoga exercises and some pushups," says Billy. "If I have time, I'll do vocal exercises. Then I answer and check e-mails and return phone calls." Since his schedule varies from day to day, Billy rarely maintains a set sleep routine. "What time I get up depends on when I go to bed," he says. "If I go to bed late, after 3:00 a.m., I won't get up until noon, but sometimes I get up at eight or nine. My sleep can be erratic. I don't have a regular sleep and waking pattern." If he has to play a gig that day, he adjusts the amount of time he sleeps. "Typically, a gig starts between 9:00 and 10:00 p.m. I'll stay up until about 5:00 or 6:00 p.m. and try to get a nap before the gig. A nap is essential. It's part of the preparation process," he says. The details for his performance are a little more flexible. "I figure out what I'll wear at the last minute." Billy's signature is a fedora hat, which he always wears during a performance. So he selects from his collection of about fifty hats and coordinates his outfit from there. The set list is pretty well established with his band, the Sons of the Blues. They typically open with "Son of Juke," a contemporary update of Little Walter's rollicking instrumental, "Juke." The John Lee Hooker classic "Boom Boom" is also usually featured.

"We know the set list by rote," he says. "We have a framework that we work from, and if I feel like doing something else, I can. I never write out a set list because I always end up changing it. The blues is best played spontaneously," he says. Billy stresses that there are certain characteristics required to be a blues musician. "You have to have tenacity, a lot of patience and a high level of tolerance," he insists. "You have to be very adaptable to situations. You need flexibility to be successful. This is not a nine-to-five; at any given moment so many things can go wrong, but 'the show must go on.'" In terms of talent and skill, Billy believes that musicians have to cultivate both, as well as learning how to connect with an audience. "You should strive to be the best musician you can be. But the bottom line is that this is show business; people want to be entertained. No matter how technically skilled you are as a musician, the person who entertains and connects to the audience will always get the most applause. You come to the realization that everyone is unique in their own right. You always strive to be the best that you can."

Noted for his lively shows, where he might roam through the audience, playing harp and talking to fans, Billy's performances draw a mix of young and seasoned blues fans. His booking agent makes calls and negotiates gigs, but Billy already has a working relationship with some clubs. "I've been doing this for close to forty years. We've been playing for decades in some clubs, so the setup is less formal." A veteran of the varied Chicago blues club scene, Billy says that each club offers a different experience. "The most energetic and animated audience is at the Kingston Mines," he says. "It's a young crowd, and they love to dance, which is wonderful. Blues should be danced to. I encourage people to dance at my gigs because it enhances the experience. When an audience is enthusiastic, it has an effect on the performer. It's a two-way street—you give the audience a great show, and they give great feedback, and you feed off each other. At Rosa's, we tend to get the real Sons of the Blues fans. It's generally a more mature audience. They come specifically to see us play. At Kingston Mines, they come for the experience; they might not even know who's playing."

Billy recalls that his experience performing at the legendary Artis' Lounge for twenty-eight years every Monday night was still another situation. "Playing at Artis' was like a communal event," he explains. "It was like a big party with no constraints. We'd play whatever we wanted."

For the rest of the day, Billy usually has meetings, social media updates and more calls. He also occasionally teaches harmonica lessons for adult students over Skype, instructing another generation on the principles of Chicago blues harp. He'll also sometimes have residencies for the "Blues in the Schools" program, where he and his band teach students in local schools blues history and music. As a former high school and college gymnast, he's pretty health conscious. If he can squeeze time in during the day, Billy will complete an extended workout routine. "I'll go to the health club and do fifteen to twenty minutes on the Stairmaster, sometimes I'll do one hundred sit-ups, curling machines, sixty-five minutes on the elliptical, the sauna, a swim and then the steam room. As you get older, the only thing to preserve your health is exercise and diet."

If there's any free time, he'll read sci-fi novels, listen to vintage radio mystery shows or play chess online with people from all over the world. "I'm a chess addict," he confesses. He'll also try to make time for songwriting on a regular basis. With twelve albums under his belt and almost two hundred guest recordings, Billy is always thinking of new song concepts.

Billy prepares to perform with another short ritual. "In a concert setting, I'll do vocal warm-ups sometimes," he says. "If it's a big show, I'll get psychologically prepared. Every performance is important. Valerie Wellington [the late Chicago blues diva] once told me that you're only as good as your last performance because it may very well be your last performance." He also enjoys playing in different types of venues. "There's something to be said about an intimate connection with the audience in a small club," he says. "With a huge concert, there's the awareness that you've attracted that many people to see you."

After his tours and local shows, fans can be counted on to make memorable comments. "I get 'That's the first time I ever heard the blues' a lot, and 'I don't like the blues but I like what you play,'" he says. " The most touching comment was when we were in Mexico and a young lady said, 'Because of you and your music, I know God exists.' You never know the effect you're having on people. Blues is the most powerful music on the planet. It's the most visceral."

Billy has witnessed the effect of that power most vividly in Latin America. "My most heartfelt audiences are in Latin America," he says. "It doesn't hurt that I can speak some Spanish. The people are so sincere and humble. Four guys came down from Chile to Argentina to hear us play. They drove for twenty-four hours and didn't have a hotel; they stayed in their car. Some of the experiences with the audiences are so phenomenal. They're so thrilled you came. For a moment, you feel like you're the Rolling Stones or somebody. The response is incredible."

A burning question among many blues fans and beginning musicians is whether you have to experience feeling the blues to be able to play the music effectively. Billy thinks that the question is fundamental to understanding the blues. "Depending on your definition of the blues, it can include the mundane as well as the esoteric," he says. "The blues can be, you're on your way to the most important job interview of your life and your car breaks down. Or it could be that your best friend took the person you love. Everyone experiences the blues. It's the only music that also describes a feeling. You can't say you have the jazz or you have the hip-hop, you have the classical. Everyone has tragedy, everyone has loss. Being poor isn't exclusive to black people. Everyone experiences obstacles."

As for the difficulties of being a blues musician, Billy can narrow it to two main issues. "One of the hardest things is having produced a sizeable volume of recorded work and not being able to hear it on a mainstream outlet. The other is getting paid commensurate with your stature, which is related to a general lack of respect that we're faced with," he says. The lack of respect relates directly to poor or unfair pay scales, which create dire situations for many blues musicians, especially the elderly. "We shouldn't have to have benefits to bury blues musicians and get medical care. That should not be. It's just wrong," insists Billy. The years of knowing one another and performing together have created a camaraderie that overshadows the competitive nature of the business, ultimately forming a tight-knit community that supports one another. "It's inspiring," says Billy, "the support that we do instinctively, without direction. When we need each other, we're there."

Bibliography

Bowers. Jane, "I Can Stand More Than Any Little Woman My Size: Observations on the Meaning of the Blues of Estelle 'Mama' Yancey." *American Music* 1, no. 11 (Spring 1993).

Edwards, David Honeyboy. *The World Don't Owe Me Nothing: The Life and Times of Delta Bluesman David Honeyboy Edwards*. Chicago: Chicago Review Press, 1997.

Grossman, James, Ann Durkin Keating and Janice Reiff. *Encyclopedia of Chicago*. Chicago: University of Chicago Press, 2004.

Herzhaft, Gerald. *Encyclopedia of the Blues*. Fayetteville: University of Arkansas Press, 1997.

Opie, Frederick Douglass. *Hog and Hominy: Soul Food from Africa to America*. New York: Columbia University Press, 2010.

Plath, James. "Queen of the Blues: Koko Taylor Talks about Her Subjects." *Clockwatch Review* (1994–95).

Reisman, Bob. *I Feel Good: The Life and Times of Big Bill Broonzy*. Chicago: University of Chicago Press, 2012.

Rowe, Mike. *Chicago Blues: The City & the Music*. New York: Da Capo Press, 1973.

———. *Chicago Breakdown*. London: Drake Publishers, 1975.

Sonnier, Austin M. *A Guide to the Blues: History, Who's Who, Research Sources*. Westport, CT, 1994.

Taylor, Frank, and Gerald Cook. *Alberta Hunter: A Celebration in Blues*. New York: McGraw-Hill, 1985.

Wilkerson, Isabel. *The Warmth of Other Suns*. New York: Vintage Books, 2010.

Yeates-Cummings, Rosalind. "Sweet Home." *Illinois Entertainer*, 2012.

Index

About the Author

Rosalind Cummings-Yeates is a journalist and arts critic with the same Chicago and Mississippi roots that helped create the Chicago blues. She holds a BS in mass communications from Illinois State University and an MS in journalism from Roosevelt University. She writes a monthly

Courtesy of Floyd Webb.

blues column, "Sweet Home," for the *Illinois Entertainer.* Her other publication credits include *Hemispheres*, MSN, *Salon*, *Woman's Day*, *Brides*, *Go Magazine*, *Yoga Journal*, *Relish*, *Home & Away*, *Chicago Reader*, Allmusic. com, *Chicago Sun Times* and *Mojo* (where she interviewed Buddy Guy about his influence on Jimi Hendrix). She has also been an adjunct professor at Columbia College–Chicago for over ten years. Rosalind is a member of the American Society of Journalists and Authors and the Society of American Travel Writers.